W9-ANK-854

Florilegium

of texts from

MOTHER MARIA CELESTE CROSTAROSA

Selected by Sabatino Majorano, CSSR

ONE LIGUORI DRIVE • LIGUORI, MO 63057-9999 • (314) 464-2500

ISBN 0-89243-574-7
Library of Congress Catalog Card Number: 93-77661

CONTENTS

Sources Cited 6

Foreword 7

Introduction 9

I.   THE DESIGN OF THE FATHER....................11

II. RESPONSE OF THE REDEMPTORISTINE
     COMMUNITY 35

     a. Faith 37

     b. Charity 45

     c. Hope 61

     d. Chastity..64

     e. Poverty 75

     f. Obedience..79

     g. Liturgy..86

     h. Prayer 97

     i. Recollection 105

     *l. Conversion and Penance......................110

     m. Humility and Meekness.......................119

     n. Love of the Cross 132

     o. Fraternal Community............................143

III. FIDELITY TO PROFESSION.......................151

     *Note: Italian alphabet does not have
     letters "j" and "k."

SOURCES CITED

ABBREVIATIONS IN ENGLISH TEXT

Autobiographia
Ed. by B. D'Orazio, Casamari, 1965

Autobiography

Sopra l'Evangelo di S. Matteo
Esercitio di amore di Dio per
tutti i giorni del anno .....

Exercise of Love
 for Every Day

Per il mese di Decembre. Eser-
citu spirituali per ogni anno

Spiritual Exercises
for December

Giardinetto interno del
divin amore.....

The Little Garden

Distinzione di molti gradi
di orazione....
Cyclostyled ed. by
D. Capone, Scala, 1968

Degrees of Prayer

Istituto e Regole del SS.mo
Salvatore condenute nei Santi
Evangelii, – secondo la versione
del codice Foggiano II e la
trascrizione di S. Majorano,
L'Imitazione..., Roma, 1978,
142-200.

Rules

Tratenimenti dell'anima
col suo Sposo Gesu...
Cyclostyled ed. by D. Capone
and S. Majorano, Scala, 1981.

Colloquies

FOREWORD TO THE ENGLISH EDITION

Father Sabatino Majorano, CSSR, arrived at the second General Assembly of the Order of the Most Holy Redeemer (1983) with a copy of the *Florilegium* for each of the delegates. It was the task of each language group to have the text translated from the original Italian into its own language. Father J. McGrath, CSSR, took on the responsibility of having the translation done for the English-speaking nuns of the Order. At his request, Father Michael Bailey, CSSR, began the work and got two-thirds of the way through (Nos. 1-79) before he had to return to Ireland because of failing health. Meanwhile, Father McGrath passed away. The job remained unfinished until Father Joseph Oppitz, CSSR, agreed to complete it.

The texts selected by Father Majorano were arranged in line with the 1975 text of the Constitutions. Some changes were made by the delegates at the 1983 meeting in preparing the final version of the Constitutions, which were approved in 1985. However, it is still possible to follow the excerpts from the writings of Venerable Maria Celeste in the order found in the Italian *Florilegium* and retained in this English edition.

The Redemptoristines of the English-speaking monasteries are grateful to Father Majorano, for his work of compiling the *Florilegium*; Father Bailey and Father Oppitz, the translators; Father John O'Donnell, chairman of the Permanent Commission for Redemptorist Spirituality, who allowed us to use the part of the text (Nos. 1-79) as published in *Readings in Redemptorist Spirituality, Volume. 2;* and all who helped put this companion to our renewed Constitutions into our hands.

It is our hope that this little volume will also be a means of spreading the knowledge of our Venerable Mother Maria Celeste and her writings.

Sister Margaret Banville, OSSR
Esopus, New York

INTRODUCTION

The Commission for the OSSR, at its meeting in November 1981, entrusted me with the task of selecting texts from Mother Maria Celeste Crostarosa that inform the renewed Redemptoristine Constitutions, in preparation for the international meeting in June 1983.

Some monasteries had, in fact, urged that there should be a more telling presence of Crostarosan statements in the renewed text of the Constitutions. Since, however, it was not possible to insert numerous quotations from Mother Maria Celeste in the text of the Constitutions, the Commission thought that a Florilegium of the most important texts from her writings — to serve as a companion to the Rule — would be the best way to facilitate the meaningful reading of the new Constitutions in the light of the charisma that graced the beginnings of the OSSR.

What follows is only a first draft that should be sifted, improved, corrected, and finalized.

My thanks to the Sisters of Scala, whose cooperation enabled me to complete the work.

In regard to the selection of texts I have made, note the following:

a. The passages chosen follow the sequence of matter in the chapters of the renewed Constitutions. This should facilitate reference to them with a view to reading the text of the Rule with deeper understanding.

b. The Crostarosan texts of the Rules are given first place and then passages from her other writings.

c. Some passages (especially those taken from the Rules) are lengthy because it did not seem possible to summarize them, given the style of Crostarosa, or because of the valuable content of the passage in question.

d. Every extract begins with a reference both to the original from which it is taken and to the edition, if there be such — even in cyclostyle form (in the event of the latter the page is given in parentheses). The works referred to are listed at the beginning of the *Florilegium.*

Finally, the reader will, of course, evaluate these extracts by the norms of the category of writing to which they belong. Crostarosa is not writing an academic theological treatise. Her category of writing is devotional. This has a decidedly mystical turn, and the language used is the effusive language of the heart of a gifted personality.

S. Majorano, CSSR

I. THE DESIGN OF THE FATHER

1. Rules, Objective, and Idea, lr-lv (150 ff)

With desire I have desired to give my Spirit to the world and to communicate it to my creatures endowed with reason, in order to live with them and in them until the end of the world.

I have given them, out of immense love, my Only Begotten Son and I have by him, given them my divine Spirit the Consoler to make them divine in life, in justice, and in truth, and to bind them all to me in love, in him who is the Son of my love, the Word himself. This is eternal life through him.

The world was made by my Divine Word and through him all things live: in him is life, and he is the essence and life of everything that has been created, and all things are in him and by means of him are alive with love and charity in myself.

So that my creatures, then, might keep in mind the never ending love with which I have loved them, it has been my good pleasure to choose this Institute to make of it a *living memorial ("Viva Memoria")*, for all the people of the world, of all that it pleased my Only Begotten Son to do for their salvation in the course of the thirty-three years he spent on earth as a mortal man. And his works are always alive before me and they are of infinite value.

Therefore, you, the souls I have chosen for this enterprise, will be glorified with him on the day of eternity.

Consequently, stamp on your spirit the features of his life and the resemblance to him that comes from imitation. *Be, on earth, living and inspired portraits of my beloved Son*, and have him only as your head and your resource.

And you will carry him about as the Life of your heart, as the Goal of your existence, as the Shepherd of your flock, and as the Master of your spirit.

Your life will be regulated by the truths taught by him in the Gospels. There are hidden all the treasures of the heavens, there is the fountainhead of life where the people, while still on their earthly pilgrimage, partake of the eternal riches of the dear Son of my love, in whom all have their existence and their life.

And just as he has glorified me in you, so be you glorified in me through him!

Let your spirit, then, live in my Divine Love, while giving to my Only Begotten all the glory and the honor. Let nobody dare usurp the title of founder or foundress of this Order, for to my Only Begotten alone does this title belong. Meanwhile, he shall be the Captain of our souls. It is he who will obtain for you, and breathe into you the Spirit, the Consoler who will enlighten you and fill you with his gifts and virtues.

And as long as you carry out my Will, I promise to make a great number of my elect and dear friends flower in this Order. These, united to my dear Only Begotten Son and transformed into his life, will be my very dear children in him: children of light and of benediction who will bear fruit until the end of the world.

And for this purpose they must be very observant of the following Rules, without transgressing the least one of them, that so their descendants may be blessed, as I have promised....This is my Will and this is my good pleasure that you be a *memorial* of me and of the works of salvation performed by me, for love of you, during my life.

Behold the culmination of these Rules given to you by my Spirit: the nine rules of virtues prescribed by me, together with my own words out of the Gospels. And they are nine in number to correspond to the nine months I spent in the womb of my mother.

2. Autobiography, 67 (127)
On the Rogation Days of April 1725, the religious in question, after receiving Communion, experienced in her soul again that transmutation of her being into that of our Lord Jesus Christ. There and then she benefited from all the precious blessings of the life of our Lord Jesus Christ; they were stamped on her soul and then she heard the Lord say to her that this mark was stamped not on her heart alone, but on the souls of the many who, through her, would have life in him.

And then she was given to understand that the Lord would establish a new Institute in the world by means of her; and that all the regulations of their life and their Rules were contained in him, in his life, as in an open book written by the totally perfect God all at once. All is contained in him, the Divine Lamb.

3. Autobiography, 70 (133)

He pointed out to her soul the whole method and manner of the details noted in the Rules. At the same time, he said to her...that it was his wish that she live in his Life, and that as a sign that the Work was his, he would give her a very great longing to suffer insults and endure hardships for love of him — and have pleasure in and taste for these hardships — and that she would have a hunger and a longing to suffer more for him; but furthermore that he would receive as done to himself all the good and the bad treatment meted out to her by others.

And, consequently, she must change her life into that of his, so that she might enable him to be reborn to the world in the souls of his dear ones, thus supplying a true testimony of those works of salvation which he had accomplished for love of mankind.

4. Colloquies III, 18 (28)

In my Omnipotence, in my Wisdom, in my Goodness, in my Justice, in my Infinity, in the revelation of my Purity, I call you, dear soul, because I want you to be clothed with all the things that make me beautiful, thus you will be the image of me and I shall live a life of love in the world by dwelling in your heart.

My beloved, I will disclose to you the treasures enclosed in all the actions of my life in its human condition united to the Word.

5. Colloquies III, 23 (35)

You ask of me, on this feast (of Christmas), that you become my perfect image, and I grant you this wish.

Enter into my Divine Heart and live there every day of your life so as to be able to achieve a true imitation of me in love and in activity through a new life witnessed by the whole world, because you are, from among many others, my only and dearly beloved.

6. Spiritual Exercises for December, med. 3

Daughter of my Divine Spirit...I formed you in time by an act of my Omnipotence. And you received this from me as your Creator and Father. You were created by my Divine Son in his eternal wisdom, and the Third Person formed you in my image by an action of love and of divine conformity with my Will. You received your being at the time decided by me, and to your natural body was fitted your immortal soul, which is a living copy and faithful portrait of my divine essence in the triad of its spiritual powers; namely, memory, intellect, and will, so that I might find myself in you, and you recognize yourself in me, your God, through faith...so that I might find myself sculptured in you so as to love myself in you and accomplish in you the purpose of your creation. And it was an act of infinite love and majesty to elevate you to the lofty heights of being eternally like to God...so that you might acquire in your soul the treasures of merit gained from imitating my Son made man and thus enable me to find my delight in you.

7. Colloquies IX, 92 (99)

My Daughter, I am an absolutely perfect being of maximum simplicity, in whom are contained all the virtues; for in me there is one sole being and one sole substance and fullness, one sole totally simple virtue in which all the virtues — the moral virtues and the others — are included.

And starting with these moral virtues, you see that I was humble, obedient, patient, enduring as well as all the other virtues, and I made a comely bouquet of them, in my human existence, for my dear spouse....

I always had patience because I waited for the sinner for ages. I was obedient and humble because I descended from heaven to earth to assume a human body in obedience to the bidding of my Father. I was humble in lowering my Divinity below my poor Humanity, with so much suffering from poverty and from affronts voluntarily endured, and endured still even now in the sacramental species of the Eucharist so many humiliations at the hands of ungrateful men....

8. Colloquies IX, 104 (109)

He the Spouse: Daughter of my heart most pure, you want to know how you can give me more satisfaction and glory in this world. I tell you for your benefit and the benefit of others: it is precisely through the observance of the Rule given you by me, that thus you would be a *living memorial* of my Life, and that it (the Rule) would be observed by those religious in my own Spirit which is in them.

Receive, O Daughter, the spirit of your Institute and graft it onto every soul that wants to receive it and be united to me, through you, by love.

Now, know well that I am conducting you at all times so marvelously by the simplicity of love; you should enter, in this same loving way, into being a *memorial of my Life* at all of the times prescribed in your and my Rule: that means that you are to live in my Spirit and be a remembrance of the actions themselves of my Life on earth.

Therefore, in every hour of the day, you will lovingly linger over one of the actions of my Life at the time prescribed by the Rule; and in this exercise you will receive such an abundance of grace, gifts, virtues, and union with me that you will be raised, without any limits, to the heights of the Divinity and to sublime levels of contemplation.

Daughter, I shall be the light of your actions, and your soul will eat the living food of that eternal life that is wrapped within the works of my Life performed when I was only on my earthly journey. This is the spirit of your Institute: to be the *living memorial is to be a living imitation of me, as though I were alive within you.*

Your life consists in filling the role of Mary Magdalene in holy contemplation: blessed will be those religious who will observe with loving vigilance, at every appointed time, the *memorial of me.* My actions and my Life will be their resting place. These are the beloved doves that nest in the hollow of the corner-stone where the hawk of hell cannot reach them and devour them.

And let each one know that the sign and seal by which I will recognize my children of this Institute is: have they observed the pre-scribed exercises as *memorials* of me.

There are two foundations on which the Rules you are embracing are based. They are based on my life, that is, on my humility and on my love. On humility because this is one of the two divine and marvelous acts which is hidden in the bosom of my Father.

What is the meaning, do you think, of what I said in my Gospel: "Learn of me that I am meek and humble of heart?...I wanted to say nothing other than to reveal to you a most sublime secret: *I am the heart of the Father* whom he sent into the world to communicate to his creatures the truth about himself."

As confirmation of this, recall what I said in my Gospels: "I have manifested to you every-thing I have heard from my Father." This means that all the hidden things of my Divinity are contained in my Holy Gospels. Accordingly, I said: *"Qui potuit capere capiat* (let him understand it who can), for every-thing is contained and revealed in the Gospels."

Therefore, the *heart of the Father is his Divine Word,* and this Heart has been his delight from all eternity.

He sent me into the world and set forth his Heart as a model of his creatures, as a model of truth, and in this he demonstrated two things that prove the infinite perfection of his Divine Being: one was the infinite love with which he took pity on his creatures and rescued them from their misery and ignorance, by redeeming them in so noble a manner; the second was his disabusing them of the falsehood and lies that the poisonous serpent, Lucifer, had sown in their minds under false pretenses, to ensnare them in ruin and lead them to paths of vice, diametrically opposed to the truth. He depicted for them a god of his own whose greatness they could acquire, thus becoming like to me by ways altogether dissimilar to my ways.

9. Rules, Spirit, 9v-12v (193ff)

It must be made clear what the spirit of this Institute is and how the Lord has been pleased to found and establish it on self-contempt and abnegation of self.

It is very important that the religious called by the Lord to observe the present Rules should know what is the spirit of their Institute, in order to exert themselves to acquire it with the help of the grace of Our Lord.

First of all, they should know that our Lord Jesus Christ, since he has been pleased to found this Institute and its Rules on the *imitation of his most holy Life,* wishes that this his work should be accomplished in those he selected in the beginning when the Order was founded.

He arranged that it should be founded on his exemplary humiliations.

And to this end he willed to establish the foundations of his Order on the contempt of self of those elected to begin his work. For, in addition to the many sufferings, difficulties, and contradictions they endured, the Lord willed that, in their contempt of self before every type of person, they would be held in derision, scorned, abused, and reviled so much that they would lose every one of the glories of self-esteem before the world and become a laughing stock in the eyes of people of every class. And it was in this setting of self-contempt that he founded this Order.

Consequently, the progress of the religious of the Most Holy Savior consists in bringing to perfection their contempt of self, and in the most profound and exemplary humiliations of the Eternal Word, Man-God, and in denial of self, in order to be better disposed for the perfect union of their soul with the Man-God himself.

And just as he came to unite himself with our human nature to accomplish this most perfect and sublime union of the soul with God, (conversely) he would also receive such an admirable work of his divine love into himself, God-Man. It was in himself that he wanted to accomplish this great marvel of his infinite charity. He wanted so to unite together these two natures that God could be called man and man be ca''ed God: how admirable and astounding this excess of divine charity!

And to make our human nature adequately disposed for this union of himself with us his most vile creatures, he willed to assume our human state and make it holy in himself and make it capable of receiving a gift that is beyond our understanding, an excess of his Divine Goodness and Mercy.

It is right for us, then, to be united to this Head, as a member of this Mystical Body, without any discrepancy or deformity. But we must go forward united together and transformed by the actions of his most holy life, with which we identify, in a way that enables us to say, as the glorious apostle of the gentiles said: *"I live, now not I, but Christ lives in me"* (Gal 2:20).

But to attain to this divine union and be one with and transformed in Jesus Christ, we must gear ourselves to walk in the footsteps of our Lord Jesus Christ, who was willing to be humiliated so much to remedy our pride and heal our infirmities, though he had no need to be humiliated.

We must, then, hold our course on this way so that all of us may be united to God in Jesus, Man and God, in a way that the Life of our Lord Jesus Christ becomes our life in God and our life becomes the only Life of Jesus Christ.

Therefore, to know what the soul must do and what should be its disposition in order to arrive at this divine union, and what should be the spirit of their vocation, it is required that their life should be lived in his

Life, and that the works they do should be united with the works of Jesus Christ our Lord — everything united totally in him.

It is necessary immediately and above everything else to enter into his admirable humiliations.

Let us look a little on our Divine Savior: what were his pathways, what was his Life, of what nature was his Spirit, and what did he do to bring about such a union?

Since he was perfect from the first instant of his Incarnation, and since his sacred humanity was united to the Word, which is the essence of holiness, and was conceived of the Holy Spirit, he had no need of humility and had no fear of vain glory.

But in this way not only did he decide to supply us with a most effective medicine for the healing of our infirmities, but he wished also to provide for his sacred humanity the very deep and sublime foundation for a sanctity of surpassing excellence.

And in his Divine Wisdom his design for the spiritual edifice of the souls chosen by him had its foundations totally on himself. He wanted himself to be our cornerstone, in order to delineate in us his divine perfections already stamped on his most sacred humanity, in order to communicate them and deploy them in all of us united to him by grace.

But what is more admirable and astounding, and is an abyss in which the angels still get lost, is that humiliation he underwent as God when, in the first instant of his Incarnation, he lowered himself to take human flesh, and, though God, became a man: "But he emptied himself taking the form of a servant and being in the likeness of man was in aspect found as man" (Phil 2:7). This was the humility of the Divine Person and is called the Divine perfection of humility. In this, no human creature could imitate him.

But he wished to take human nature and in it to arrange and communicate to our human nature a participation in these Divine perfections. To this end, the Word traced out in the most holy soul of our Lord Jesus Christ the perfect fullness of this most excellent perfection in order to bestow it on the whole of humankind, that is, on all those souls who are united to him and enjoy the fruits of this divine union of love and become the heirs of his grace. To show us the way and the route to this happy state of union with Jesus in God and to participation in the divine perfections through participation in and union with the Life of Jesus, he announces that we must travel in the footsteps he traveled in his most holy Life.

To this end, he appears in the world as a poor man, vile and despised, who hides his Divinity under the form of a weak infant in the loneliness of a crib, known only to three poor shepherds, with a little straw for a bed, in a stable among animals. He feigns fear of the persecuting Herod and flees into Egypt. He does not avail of any miracle for himself, but hastens as a frail fugitive to a foreign land. There he remains, hidden and unknown, in painful poverty.

This most Holy Soul remains at the beck of the Divine Will, without regard to what he wanted or did not want. The Will of God alone reigns supreme in this loving Heart, poor and despised by men, unknown and hidden in God. On this perfect humility he raises the glorious throne of his humiliations and lays the foundation of Christian perfection in human nature. And as our Leader he rejoiced in a life of contempt of self for thirty-three years of his most holy Life. And he wanted to be despised by men and to allow his divine doctrine to be calumniated. He allowed himself to be mocked and persecuted by all sorts of people and be the subject of vile contempt. He hid his miracles, forbidding others to talk about them and not wanting them to be publicized.

He was hidden in God and lived until death in disregard for himself and died enduring insults, sorrows, and pains, without having recourse to any miracle, hidden in God, the perfect person-ification of infinite humility. And what of us who are his members, united to him as our Leader? He transforms and changes us into a new creature in God, united to him by grace; transmits to us and gives us a share in his divine perfections. And this soul which walks with him arrives at the point of possessing the divine union of Jesus in God.

Consequently, the religious of the Order can well see what the spirit of their vocation is because this Divine Master decided to be the founder of the Order himself. They are called to the greatest perfection that can be imag-ined, because he — our Head Legislator, and Guide — wants the members united to him to be adorned with those divine perfections which he our Head has in himself as a man united to the Divine Person — a man transformed into a new creature in God.

They should, then, aspire to a total death to every form of glory and of worldly esteem and seek to fix themselves in the depths of the admirable humiliations of the Word, the Eternal Wisdom.

They should base their spiritual edifice firmly on this absolutely unshakable cornerstone, and on contempt for themselves and for all created things, despising the world and all its honors, despising oneself as worthless in one's own heart and as vile in one's own eyes, hiding oneself in Jesus who is himself hidden in God and burying oneself in the humiliations of the Word, burying oneself in the hiding place of the Man-God hidden beneath his self-emptying, liking the fact of being despised by every person in the world. Just as our Divine Master so desired contempt of self that he wanted to live and die despised, disapproved of by the leaders of Judea; not only that, but he wanted to be despised even by the whole throng of ordinary people in the magnificent city of Jerusalem.

He hid all the glory of his Divinity and buried it beneath his perfect humility and contempt of self, through life and at death, because the first man sinned through greedy ambition to win honor for self and through a loathing for humiliations, so he (the New Man), by means of humiliations and contempt of self, a Man united to the Divine Person of the Word, undertook to unite to God all those who were predestined. And he undertook, by means of his self-contempt, to restore to God that honor which man owed him in justice, since he was both Man and God. And more than that — he brought it about that the human person, united to his Life, would participate in those divine perfections which he, because of his sacred humanity, participated in; and thus he shared the good things that were his with us his brothers and sisters.

Therefore the religious of the Order of the Most Holy Savior should begin her journey and continue on it until she arrives at contempt of self, by keeping her eyes fixed on this God made Man, the true Life of her soul, by disdaining all disorderly affections, by denying herself continually and always despising bad and evil inclinations — the bad habits of the old Adam, putting them to death in Christ who was mortified and crucified. Her way is the way of contempt for self, and of dying repeatedly to the disorderly affections of her carnal self in all the appetites of the rebellious senses and of the predominant passions, because the Divine Savior, in his own words in the Holy Gospel, declares that if the seed of grain which falls on the ground does not die, it remains alone, and cannot bear fruit for life eternal (Jn 12:24).

And in saying this, he not only intended to explain to his disciples his Passion and Death, but he wished to teach us and explain to us how to walk his spiritual way:

he would have us know that it is in him, God-Man, that we would accomplish perfectly the work of dying totally to the old Adam, in order to remodel ourselves on him and thus be transformed into a new creature, through a loving union with him in God.

For this purpose he willingly instituted the Sacrament of the Altar and thereby his Divine Love devised another divine invention which is more stupendous and admirable than anything our minds can imagine. How can any human words describe this humiliation, this stowing away of self, since it involves a refinement of divine love that goes beyond understanding? To humiliate oneself to the point of becoming the food of human kind, food that is substantial, real and divine.

All this he did for the sole purpose of transforming the human person into God and of communicating to her his divine perfections. He wished that the human person would, by means of this food of life, be nourished by the flesh of that Lamb, become a holocaust in the ashes of his supreme divine humiliations; and that the old Adam in us would die in his death: by undergoing self-abasement, by reducing ourselves to nothingness in him to the point of being dead, through abasement of self, to everything — our honor, our self-esteem, our own will, our own judgment, our own wisdom. Because this our God gave us an example of humiliation in his shameful death, not only on the occasion of his birth and throughout his most holy life but even after his glorification as he now sits at the right hand of God the Father, he has willed to find an admirable way of most perfect humility which can be called the divine perfection of humility. For he decided to give himself as food to the human person under the accidents of bread, to remain present there in hiding, subjecting himself to so many insults from ungrateful men, and humiliating himself by obeying the simple words of every priest, be he worthy or unworthy without exception, solely out of the excess of his Divine Love.

From this we conclude that his humility, not only as Man but as Man-God, has attained an infinite perfection which is beyond our understanding.

And, consequently, every religious of this Institute should know that she has not been called by God for any other purpose but to die to her own will.

By making her profession, the soul, through the vow of obedience renounces self and becomes buried to the world; she gives all the signs of being dead to everything she possesses, declaring herself to be buried in Christ and dead in Christ to all the activities of her unregenerated self. And the presiding Prelate (explaining the symbolism of the ceremony) says that in rising from the ground, she rises in Christ alive in God, because she, at the time, by that burial (prostration) declared that she wished for the future to walk not now according to the will of the flesh, nor according to her own wishes, but according to the Spirit of Jesus Christ. Hence she says: *"For me to live is Christ and to die is gain"* (Phil 1:21): she is saying that her life is the dead Christ and that for her to die is a gain.

But this death and this life are not brought about immediately by formally pronouncing these words during the ceremony; they are realized every day and every hour of the life of a good observant religious in the measure that the soul will be diligent, at all times and on every occasion, in living always in death to herself, to all her own activities that derive from her unregenerated nature. And in the measure that she will live this death to self she will have life in Christ...And then she can say with Christ in God. "I come not to do my own will, but the will of him who sent me" (Jn 6:38), not in word merely, but in works which bear fruit of eternal life, in Christ her true Life.

And then the soul has truly achieved the purpose for which God called her to this vocation and obtains true Life in Christ and can say: *"I live, now not I, but Christ lives in me"* (Gal 2:20).

Here the soul is buried in the humiliations of the Word, God-Man; with contempt for self she enters into his humiliations. Since Jesus is the divine treasurer of the Eternal Father, he places them all, marked with the seal of his Humanity, in God. In him all the treasures of heaven are to be found, and he has given to man a share in his divine perfections in Jesus, but he has stamped these with his own humiliations and contempt of self. He was buried among the disgraced. He submerged his divine immensities beneath an admirable hidden silence while on earth as a *Wayfaring Man,* and not only that, but now while hiding — in the Most Holy Sacrament of the Altar, beneath the accidents of bread — his divine grandeurs, he is still subjected to so many insults by bad Christians. And to unite us with him and transform us into God he has made himself the real food of man.

He wished to live and die in contempt of self, and now that he is in glory, still undergoing humiliations sublime beyond all telling, he unites himself to us in this most divine Sacrament through an astonishing act of humiliation, in order that the soul, his Spouse, might live and be transformed into the Divine Life by receiving the fullness of the fruits of these Divine perfections and live the life of Jesus in God.

Who can understand the depth of this fact and this humility? He wished to feed us with his Immaculate Flesh in order to graft on us the divine perfections which he, being at the same time God and Man, possessed in himself. We are united to him in such a close and real union that when the soul has received him in this most divine Sacrament, she can speak of herself as a living God by participation. But the soul must despise self and totally annihilate everything that belongs to her natural self, whatever is not of God.

Why, if she does not remove all those things that are repugnant to this most perfect Divine Being, is she unable to arrive at this perfect union of love of Jesus in God? It is because Jesus destroyed these things in himself, burying them beneath his humiliations and his admirable self in concealment and contempt of self. Because he wished to be born and live and die poor and despised, not only throughout his most holy Life while still a *Wayfarer* on earth, but even now in the Most Holy Sacrament of the Altar he is subjected to infinite insults under the species of bread: all that he suffered for love of us on earth were not sufficient for him!

To obtain this divine union and to gain this participation in his Divine Life, the soul must come into his presence and become united with Jesus — Jesus poor, humble, despised by men, buried in his ignominies, marked with insults, hidden and ignored by the world, persecuted, scoffed at by his own people, people who repaid his miracles with abuse, and the many benefits they received with ingratitude.

He submerged his divine grandeurs beneath a strict silence, hiding his omnipotent Divine Being under insults while refusing to work any miracle.

Hence the conclusion that his humiliations are the keys to the Divine treasures of the living God.

The soul must live the life of Jesus, the despised God-Man, and enter into his humiliations in order to enter the Life of God. She receives God and is received by God, receiving God into her life: the Life of love in the Holy Spirit.

And that is the spirit of our Institute to which we have been called by him to live in a union of love the same Life of the Son of Eternal Love, Word, Man-God, eternally our Life. So may it be. Amen

10. Exercise of Love for Every Day, December 3

Mary was a prodigy of graces because she was

a heroine of humility; in her the donor placed his graces in safe-keeping because certainly there was no possibility she would claim the credit for them herself.

O my Lady and Mother, well can you say that all generations in heaven and on earth will call you blessed, because you are an instrument of the Divinity, formed by God for the triumph of his mercy, wisdom, and infinite omnipotence.

You are our only Hope, all nations will call you blessed; the angels and all the heavenly spirits look on you as their Queen, since you are the Mother of the great King; the just have recourse to you as to a Rock of strength and the Teacher of virtues, safe Guide in this vale of tears, Gate of salvation; under your patronage sinners hurry to you to obtain pardon and protection from your Son, our Judge; and all generations recognize you as Mediatrix and instrument of our Redemption; and you are the terror of hell because you brought about their defeat, crushing the head of the dragon.

Grant that I may imitate you, by never attributing to myself what is not mine, and may I serve you and spend my life imitating you.

11. Exercise of Love for Every Day, December 30

Yes, my Lady, you enter into the Divine garden of God the Father, into his Word made Man, in order to draw a living Copy of the Divine Original. In you myrrh is mixed with the aromas of all the fruits of the Holy Spirit. In you myrrh is singled out because you are a genuine copy of your Son in that you (like him) suffered more than any creature. You are a true image of the Original, a portrait of Jesus. O my Mother, you are a pure crystal that sparkles most clearly.

You are the one invited into this garden, and through you all of us your friends, that is to say, all those who enter with you into the garden of his Sacred Humanity by imitating the life and virtues of Jesus and becoming genuine copies of him: these are they who with you taste the sweetness of the honey and mild and precious wine.

O Mary, Jesus wants us to resemble him, but only you have succeeded in becoming a genuine copy where Jesus, God-Man, Infant can contemplate himself and be pleased.

O Mother of fair Love, I have recourse to you: may I enter this beautiful garden of delights of the Father in Jesus your Son and grant that I may reproduce in me a perfect copy of him, and may be one of his friends who becomes inebriated by this sweetest of wines.

This is a prayer to obtain perfect imitation of Jesus Christ.

12. Exercise of Love for Every Day, December 31

Today love leads us to talk about the divine resemblance of Jesus in Mary, stamped by sacred and divine love on her heart and on her arm. He wishes to remain over her heart like a seal imprinted on her will, that is to say that his Divine Will must remain imprinted on the judgment of Mary in a way that the will of Mary becomes so faithful a resemblance of the Divine (Will) that a genuine portrait of the Divinity would seem to be carved on the heart of Mary....

His Son, Jesus, was the divine seal with which the Father stamped his image on Mary, a seal of infinite love which, by being stamped on Mary, was, through her, engraved on all our hearts as an emblem and sign of the love of God our Father in us.

In Mary a *live copy of Jesus* was brought out, having all the Christian virtues, true humility, charity, uniformity with God's Will, poverty of spirit, patience, crucifixion, and true martyrdom of love....

But in us this beautiful engraving is distorted because in us so many scars of the passions, the senses, of self-love considerably disfigure it.

This is what I see in myself, and therefore I have recourse to you, Mother of Love, so that through your intercession the live image of Jesus might be engraved on me so that my Heavenly Father might look on me with the same infinite love with which he contemplates, in himself, his Beloved and Divine Son; with the same love may he love us who are in the image of his Humanity. We pray that this be granted to us.

II. RESPONSE OF THE REDEMP-
TORISTINE COMMUNITY

13. Colloquies I, 1-2 (4-5)

Most sweet Spouse of my soul, my Lord, the only one my spirit longs for, you are in the bosom of the Eternal Father like a seal in the hands of the one who fashions it; I find you to be precisely that seal with which all just souls are stamped with the hallmark of justice and holiness. This is the seal of love with which many elect souls are stamped; with this one and only seal so many living portraits of your unique love are fashioned.

Who can sufficiently describe the nobility of the soul created by you? You have enriched it to an extent that exceeds the capacity of the human person in every respect, not because of itself, but because of your substance, since it is a participation in your being. Oh how infinitely noble is the human being created with the faculty of intelligence! The sole fact of contemplating it leaves me dumbfounded.

In virtue of my attribute of mercy...I produce every type of moral virtue. These are communicated through the Word to human nature, and through it, to all the just on earth. Out of my goodness I grant with wisdom and justice the four cardinal virtues; with omnipotence the supernatural gifts; with grace the theological virtues to all my creatures.

If anyone should ask you who am I, reply that I am love and true goodness: love in myself, love for myself, love in my creatures by means of goodness.

14. Colloquies II, 13 (20)

I want you in a special way in my heart...so that there you might be espoused to all my souls whom I have in my Church and also to those not yet in the bosom of the Church.

I want it that way in order that you might have for them that same wholehearted love that I have for them. And just as I thought more about them than about my own Person when I was on earth, so you must not think anymore about yourself, but about the salvation of the souls that I love so much.

Accordingly, I extend my right hand over to you. I bring you close to my heart so that by my embracing you, you might embrace in my Heart all my creatures; and that through my kiss of love to you, you might give to those souls the kiss of love in my Heart.

15. Colloquies VII, 51 (67)

Since his kingdom has no end, my Heavenly Father has invited all men, his vassals, to put on the garments of his only Son.

This "he has done" out of love and to raise them up to the great heights of the eternal kingdom, rejoicing at seeing "in them" the marks of my true love, that is my virtues, my beautiful qualities, and consequently making them the heirs to the very heritage of his kingdom; and this because of the grace and the clothing of charity.

But this kingdom he has placed at the discretion of human beings: of whoever wishes to be clothed with my garments, by granting him the pledge of the character of Baptism; thus he who wants to be saved is saved, and he is lost who voluntarily wants it....

a. *Faith*

16. Autobiography, 60-61 (117-118)

The Lord gave me clarity of perception, granting me knowledge of the truths of the faith with a very effective supernatural light; and drawing me to himself he showed me how he lives in the just soul and is its Life.

My Jesus, in the close union and by means of his Divine grace, has created in my soul a sweet resemblance of eternal life, enabling me to understand these words he pronounced in the Holy Gospel: *"I am the Way, the Truth, and the Life. No one comes to the Father but through me."* He showed my soul the astounding work of the union of the Divine with a human being which he has accomplished, and how the soul attains this through faith, through the grace of his Holy Spirit, and through the marvelous fruits of the good works and virtues of his most holy Life while he was a Man, as *a Wayfarer* on earth. For he has become the Way sent from heaven, the Truth by means of the gift of the virtue of faith revealed to us through a supernatural gift; and he is the Way, the Truth, and the Light of grace in our mind: he is our Life in virtue of the union of the Divine Person with the human nature, he lives in God in a union of love, he lives in all his dearly loved souls as a *Wayfarer* the Life of their life.

*** The Way comprises the works and virtues of Jesus Christ, which have become the works of the soul itself through grace; the Truth derives from the faith infused in our mind through a supernatural free gift in the soul loved by him; and the Life consists in the love and the union with the Beloved Word.

And consequently one concludes that he is a *Wayfarer* in those who are united to him through love and true union in God through faith, by means of saintly works and by the grace of the Holy Spirit.

17. Colloquies III, 18 (27)

O eternal Sweetness, until now my heart seemed to have need of some human creature to help it in its journey "toward" you. Now, oh my only Good, I do not feel that way; on the contrary, it seems to me that you are more to me than a tender mother, altogether loving and solicitous toward me more than is a tender mother toward her little son whom she holds to her breast.

Loving and dear Mother mine, what is there that I might have that I will not show to you? O my Consoler, you are at all times my all. O Word, Wisdom of the Father, you are the most learned of teachers. Your instruction brings to my mind the clarity of the Eternal Truth, in the same way that you are now declaring it to me.

Spouse: My dearly beloved soul, the Faith is one and the Truth is one: that is to say that I am the God of all truth and of all goodness. This embraces every perfection "toward which" you intend to advance. Accordingly, faith is the solid base of the soul, the point where it becomes united to my being. In this faith do thou embrace me totally in a single altogether simple act of union with my complete divine essence.

18. Colloquies VIII, 75 (86)

Look at yourself as you truly are, namely a little baby in the womb of its mother which lives more in the life of its mother than of itself. The baby does not do any work, only what its mother does, and it is nourished with the nourishment of its mother. Thus it is with you, O my Daughter.

I am your Mother, I have created you in my womb...if you should go outside of that womb, you would lack life-giving support and would perish. Every person journeying on earth is like a baby not long conceived, still in its mother's womb: if nature prematurely expels it from the mother's body, it loses its life; thus it is with the human person journeying on earth when it is separated from its life's source.

This is how I want you now: like a babe in your mother's womb! Do not wish for anything but only this womb, which created you and guards you, and you will be free from every human danger. The womb that envelops you is the abandoning of yourself to my good will, the committing of yourself to the care and the protection of your Mother. Do not think of anything else, only rest yourself totally in guaranteed safety where no evil can reach you.

Remain thus in repose in every situation: in labors, in doubts, in fears, in temptations, in preoccupations, and in humiliations attach yourself to the womb of your dear Mother. While you cling to it, no evil can reach you: *sorrow does not enter within this placenta of joy.*

I am that good which you call Goodness. While you are in me and while you nourish yourself on me, no evil will come near you inasmuch as I will nourish you on my substance. Therefore, do thou, as I do, live in loving simplicity; love the simple and lowly; do not judge my affairs according to human prudence; do not desire to go more deeply into things beyond the level I disclose to you.

*** Place yourself completely in the arms of my Divine Providence, like one carried along by a strong giant; you have no more strength than a wisp of straw in the face of a robust wind, and all creatures are similarly like straws before the wind. Live then as a babe in my womb.

19. Colloquies IX, 112 (115)
Spouse: Daughter, the faith is the Divine Truth, and I am the Light by which the eye of your mind perceives the truth of faith. These things are made manifest by my light because my Heavenly Father sent me into the world to be the light of men so that the eternal truths of the faith might become manifest to them. That is why I said that I am the Light of the world and that no one can come to the Father but through me.

The faith is nothing else but the manifestation of the truth which you see by my light; and know that this light is not obscure or dark to those who have the eyes to see by my light.

There is no faith and consequently there is no light whenever the eyes of the mind of people are in darkness because blinded by the things that are perceived by the senses and by the human mind; and hence, faith and hope and charity are dead in them and they do not see the things that are eternal because they are blinded by the things of earth.

Do thou, Daughter, renounce always the things that can be seen, felt, and known by merely human perception in order to look on me alone at all times, the Light of the eternal truths; and your eyes, thus cleansed of the things of earth, will gaze openly by my inaccessible Light at the eternal truths, and thus you will live in a faith that is alive and not dead and in hope and in charity; and your faith will be not a dark, but an illuminated, way that leads directly to heaven.

20. Colloquies IX, 143 (133)

Ah, my supreme and infinite Good, to what heights have you raised up your vile creature! And yet it is absolutely certain that if my soul should for one quarter of an hour turn away from its watch of faith and not maintain its vigilance, alert not to lose sight of you, it would without any doubt sin.

...If I do not *keep my gaze fixed on you* always, my supreme and infinite Good, it is my experience that as often as my soul is diverted to something alien, something other than you, it becomes stained. Therefore, I am not surprised that poor, worldly-minded creatures fall into so many mortal sins and miseries: once they are outside this Refuge which is so effective, it could not possibly be otherwise, because we are part of a mass so corrupt and miserable that it could not but turn out that way when the soul loses sight of you. Thus it is safe only as long as it sees you present through faith.

O happy Presence, this is the daily bread of man which you teach us to ask from the Eternal Father, every day, so that we may have life in you.

...In fact, this glance of faith at first purifies the soul of its stains; but afterward, it gives the soul the same God as food: Give us this day our daily bread (Mt 6:11).

Thus it is. And any soul desiring to arrive at perfection should not dare to attain to this by any other way than by this arduous application to the task of being always committed to contemplating with love her God present to her. And the greater her application the faster will she arrive at this perfection.

21. Degrees of Prayer I, 4 (1)
O my sweet God and Lord, help my tongue to declare how my heart feels about this most Holy Faith. I have begun indeed by climbing this first rung of the mystical ladder of this theological virtue (faith), but it points to the ascent to the final rung of faith. For, by means of this ascent, the soul is given a royal

main road forward and a sure pathway that directs her on to the union of the soul with her God.

This is the mystical ladder Jacob saw reaching from earth to heaven. The earth is the Catholic Church where the Holy Faith is planted; and consequently every Christian soul rests on this solid foundation, the cornerstone which is Christ.

The angels, whom this holy prophet saw as ascending and descending by this ladder, signify the insights and lights on the mysteries of the faith that are communicated to the soul by means of these heavenly spirits; similarly they signify the lights given to the holy Fathers and the commentators to decipher and understand the Catholic truths: it is through the light of the Holy Spirit that so many Catholic truths are revealed.

22. Spiritual Exercises for December, med. 4

Daughter of charity, aided by my light, reflect on my love for you in calling you to the state of my grace, though you had been born my enemy because of sin; reflect on the outpouring of mercy with which I espoused you to Wisdom: my Divine Spirit endowed you with his gifts and virtues, clothed you with the robe of charity which my Beloved Son merited for you by the shedding of his Blood, and he adorned you with such great gifts and graces that you have been made the heir to my eternal kingdom of glory; and the faith was infused in you and by it you became a noble and mystical creation, and the dignity to which this faith elevated you was so great that it has not been sufficiently appreciated by you.

Know well that through this faith your soul is united with my Divinity.

This faith is the Guide, which leads in darkness as regards the things of my kingdom. In this faith you have become espoused to my Divinity; and through this faith God's union of love with your soul by grace is accomplished. In virtue of this, you can possess so many good things, so many of my treasures and gifts right up to the union and consummation in the Holy Spirit of the most pure marriage in the eternity of glory, namely, the possession of God, the One and Triune, in that most holy love with which I delight in my Beloved Son, the Eternal Wisdom, in the love with which my Beloved Son contemplates himself in my creating womb, in the union of the Holy Spirit, the mysterious beloved who is defined as love most pure, in the eternal and divine essence.

Daughter, here then is where you are led by the faith which I gave you in my Baptism; walk always with this faithful escort and have no fear of any sort of deception.

Renounce everything that the world of the senses promises you, all the appearances, forms, and figures which your blind senses are drawn to dwell on and on which your passions feed.

Take refuge from them in the innermost recesses of our soul and spirit and be oblivious of every created object. In that way you will become possessed of the hidden treasure of a pure faith, the faithful escort which will conduct you to the truth and to the peace that is the kiss of the Holy Spirit. And you will arrive safely at my kingdom.

23. Degrees of Prayer II, 10 (4)

O purest truth of holy faith, how lovable and precious you are! It is you who bring all the divine treasures into the soul: in your pure quality I find my supreme Good in all its beauty.

But this view so full of love keeps me in a purgatory at once of love and of pain, because in the true light of faith the difference separating your most pure being from my being becomes clear.

And were it not for the lively confidence and hope in you, which the same faith generates in the soul, the soul would be in a serious torment in the face of the divine beauty of your being.

But, O God of my heart, the certainty which the faith communicates to the soul in that degree of prayer just discussed increases, in an admirable way, the soul's hope and confidence, without the soul understanding how it received this.

b. *Charity*

24. Rules, Charity, 5v (166-167)

"This is my commandment, that you love one another as I have loved you. Greater love than this no man hath, than that a man lay down his life for his friends" (Jn 15:12).

I descended from heaven to give myself totally to you and to give my Life not only for my friends but also for my enemies, for the glory of my Father and for your salvation; thus with the wisdom of my intelligence, I granted to human minds clouded by the darkness of sin the clarity of vision to discover the eternal truths.

I gave you my *memory* to recall for me my former mercies toward my creatures who are endowed with reason.

I gave you my Will to love you with that divine love with which I love my Heavenly Father, and to give my own Life for your eternal salvation.

This is my new commandment that you love one another reciprocally, as I have loved you. Thus you will give your whole self to your neighbor.

You will give her your intelligence, by raising up its beneficent activity to the level of my mercy; never use it to judge her, whatever evil she has done.

You will give her your memory by pardoning her from your heart and never keeping in your memory the offenses she inflicted and repaying her with spiritual and temporal favors.

You will give her your will by loving her from your heart, treating her as you would want others to treat yourself and wishing her every possible good.

You will give her your heart with its affections, for the sake of my love, sympathizing with her in her afflictions, her weaknesses, and her spiritual and corporal stresses.

You will employ your body and your senses for her benefit: your eyes to observe her needs but never to scrutinize her faults and her way of acting; do not pass judgment on her in any matter; your ears to listen to her grievances; your mouth to console her in her afflictions and to instruct her in the eternal truths where understanding of them is deficient; help her and defend her.

The substance of all this is that your body and your life should be ready to sacrifice self when charity requires this for your neighbors' salvation, so that you too would do as I have done. Glory be to God. Amen.

25. Rules, Constitutions, 21r-21v (168)

This virtue of charity to the neighbor is the principal foundation of our Institute, because Our Lord made this virtue the base on which rests the evangelical law of Christian perfection. Consequently, the sisters abstain from murmuring about the faults and imperfections of their neighbor and from rash judgments, contriving to make excuses for her action and her intention as far as possible, always putting a good interpretation on matters and never passing rash judgments on anyone. But if she should come to know of something in any sister that would be none too edifying or would be against the Rule and Constitutions, she should draw that sister's attention to the matter secretly up to three times, and if she does not change the superior should be informed.

They will be on their guard against envies, the spirit of emulation, of contradicting one another, of recriminations, of competing against one another for little trifles, of upsetting oneself over frivolous matters, and such like things that disturb charity and peace of heart.

The superior will be most diligent in mortifying and punishing failures, even in the smallest matters, in this virtue of charity, by the sisters.

In order to preserve among themselves true peace and charity, and in order to maintain a regular level of this virtue so greatly recommended by our Lord Jesus Christ, the sisters will desist from carrying stories, for example — "So and so said this about you...," or the like, which are so prejudicial to this virtue of charity.

And on this point the sisters should be very alert, because in this area it is very easy to slide into grave sin, more or less according to the matter. Here we are dealing with a commandment of Our Lord, which he inculcated so much and which he recommended to all Christians in the Holy Gospel.

26. Colloquies IX, 100 (106)

O most holy adorable Name of Jesus...a name so beautiful, so sweet, so dear, so agreeable, so great, so full, so lovable, so admirable, so divine! Let me then speak and exhale the love that is in my heart to you, with freedom and without restraint, because I tell you who are my entire Love, Life, Heart, and my very Soul.

Now, do you tell me, Beloved, why do you set my soul afire so much?

It is filled with fire; at the mere fact of hearing your name pronounced, my heart seems wounded and writhing as from a sharp sword, by this fair name.

I cannot persuade myself that there is any other soul you love more than me; all my sighs and aspirations reach out to you to wound you with the same love with which you have stricken me.

O Joy of my heart, the marrow of my bones, the Breath of my life, the Beauty of my countenance, the core of my being, my totally Loved One, how dear and how lovable you are to me!...It is for a very good reason that so many loving souls are dead out of pure love for you, and more than any other, the heart of your dear Mother, who more than any other creature, was so eminently versed in the knowledge of the Divine and in whom consequently the flame of charity burnt most brightly, to such an extent that you drew her to yourself by separating her from the temporal life of the body.

27. Colloquies IX, 123 (122)

Your thoughts, your desires, your affections, and your works will be directed to nothing else but to the exercise of my love, faithfully, and with a surpassing dynamism, fueled by the fire of charity.

You will always be on fire with a pure flame of most chaste love until finally, after all the worldliness has been burnt out of your being, *I alone am living in your life.*

You will exercise a truly free action, being careful only not to allow entrance within you of any alien thought and of any created object (in regard to this I would have you know that I am *most jealous of your heart*), if you yearn to be faithful to my love.

28. Colloquies I, 2 (6)

Every act and movement of yours that is not inspired by my love is neither virtuous nor good in you: so everything will be virtue and perfect goodness when all will be love, when everything will be my goodness.

I, being infinite virtue by essence, make reflections of myself in you since you are my image. And I love this image with that infinite love with which I love you. And I receive from you the delight of being loved with that same goodness with which I love you with infinite love.

And just as I delight in loving this image of me, so it gives me delight that it should be loved by you also, and that you should have for this resemblance to me the same love that I have for it.

Hence, I want you to become espoused to all my souls and to experience the delights in them which I experience.

Accordingly, enter, my spouse, into my Heart and admire the beauty of these images which I created in my own likeness, and be no longer surprised that I should have come down from heaven and died for them on the Cross: my own Love did all of this, because in them I have given expression to my Goodness, my Wisdom, my Omnipotence, and the intellectual quality of a pure spirit, together with all the beautiful features with which you see my Heart to be adorned.

And since I am your Spouse, you have become espoused to Love and to Goodness, now I want you to become espoused also to those who take delight in my Goodness, that is to become espoused to the souls I love. O my dear spouse, in this encompassing embrace, I hold you close to myself and you hold all my souls close to yourself: and in embracing you I clasp to my heart all those souls as I clasp you.

Thus, both I and you taste the delights that I have in them out of my immense love, without any distinction because each one means as much to me as if she were the only one, and I the only Lover of each one of them.

29. Colloquies II, 14 (20)

Since you have received my Heart into yours to love it always as you love your own heart, see to it that you hold close to you, with the bond of charity, all the souls that are mine. In a special way the souls of this community where you are living will be your dear spouses; you will love them and will have concern for their spiritual welfare; I entrust them to you, my beloved; they are my spouses and your spouses; from now on you will love them in me and me in them.

30. Colloquies II, 11 (16)

Charity resides in simplicity. I reside in frank and simple souls who regard their neighbor only to honor her, putting a good interpretation on all her actions and ascribing to her the same intentions for acting as she herself does in her simplicity; and I find my repose in them as I would the midday rest, while granting them to share in my spirit of peace.

Daughter, do thou "think" thus in a simple way about the actions of others, with the good spirit of the good intention, without "suspecting" any aim to be "astute" in the manner of acting of your neighbor, so that if there be anything unauthentic in their activities, it will not gain entry into you; and I will find in your spirit the splendor of pure simplicity lacking in the activities of your neighbor; thus you will make up for the deficiencies in those souls by means of the love in your soul. It is thus I want you to be, simple as my pure dove. That is the road along which I want to lead you.

Accordingly, whenever you prejudice this purity of intention in your spirit and your thinking, you do not find in yourself the clear radiance of familial love. Out of the love that I bear you, I cause you to feel distant from me when you neglect this purity in dealings with your neighbor, and so avoid passing any judgments on the things that are of earth, to the extent that life with others permits. "I do this" in order to liberate you from self-love which accomplishes in souls "their own interests" in the way the venomous serpent does.

In those souls who are more willingly seduced by this serpent, it is observed that for them humiliations are turned into poison, because this wounded self-love turns its venom against me and against the neighbor who is thought to have humiliated them. They take everything in bad part, they commit a thousand imperfections by way of failing to conform to my Will and of aversion to their neighbors;

and in them charity grows cold and other evils also follow from this occur.

Hence, my Daughter, watch out for and guard against this serpent and draw your neighbor's attention to it when you see her being seduced by it, so that she may not allow it a place of refuge in her spirit.

31. Degrees of Prayer VI, 48 (20)

This soul has quite pure degrees of charity because she does not love or esteem the things of earth or value such things as honors, riches, and the admiration of the world. And this soul does not voluntarily become involved in anything save what pertains to the glory of her Beloved, for whom alone she would allow herself to be broken to bits; nor does it worry her if, because of this, she should be criticized or humiliated by creatures, because, in my view, she would sooner be deprived of her own self-esteem than be deprived of those things that appertain to my Beloved.

And so here the soul becomes possessed of very great desire to do great things for God and to suffer all sorts of pain and labor for him.

She fears nothing, because in this real dream she is given very great helps. And she is not able to keep to herself anything that is useful and profitable to her neighbors.

Here is where the world very often condemns this holy audacity, for whoever does not know what spirit impels her, judges her to be presumptuous and arrogant.

But she holds firm because of her desire to suffer: and if she suffers because of this she is glad and content for the sake of her soul, because nothing in the world gives her more joy than to endure pain and suffering for her Beloved.

Her burning desires to do great things for her Beloved are so great that her greatest trial is the insignificance of what she can do to serve him because of her weaknesses.

32. Degrees of Prayer X, 78 (33)
In this chapter the most sweet Divine Master must repeat those meaningful words where he says:

"I came to cast fire on the earth."

He had already declared with his own divine lips that he came to set on fire and burn the hearts of men with the flame of the Holy Spirit.

Since then, the soul is in divine union with God the Word through love, it is often living in the pure fire of the Holy Spirit.

...Here, there is a peace which surpasses every comparison, so great is the lovable sweetness of love in God, with its most sweet destruction (of self): the soul feels an all-pervading flame that burns irresistibly and never consumes.

This, however, breaks out in praise of the beloved Lord. And the soul often pours out songs of praise and love in its longing to have a million tongues with which to praise the Lord.

This prayer has two effects on the soul: the praising of God and a deep desire to see the Lord served and loved by all creatures.

The first expresses the soul's love for the supreme Good; the second pertains to the good and the love of the neighbor, which burns brightly in the soul, as the Lord gives it a marvelous charity and activity for helping all neighbors. And so it does this so readily and energetically with a contagious love that it very sweetly instills and evokes the working of the same charity in the souls of others.

Here can be seen how this soul, without regard for its own interests, goes forward unhampered and liberated from concerns about herself, in search of the good of others in order to have more companions in love.

She willingly leaves behind the sweet enjoyments she could experience in the depths of her heart, the rest for her senses and the peace of the solitude that this results in. She would lay down her life a thousand times for the salvation of just one soul.

She hastens, full of affection, to help her neighbor in her needs be they spiritual or temporal, becoming all things to all mankind, consoling the afflicted, serving the infirm, helping and comforting the weak, instructing the ignorant in the way of salvation, and drawing sinners to repentance.

She applies herself with the whole of her energy as though she were led by a superior force, without paying attention to anyone but only to the glory of her beloved God for whom she would be glad to spend her life a thousand times over if this were possible.

She helps others to accomplish great and heroic deeds. And in this situation, her words are so powerful and efficacious in inducing others to do great things that they seem to be arrows to the heart of the one who listens to them. And because of this, the resulting benefits to the souls of others are marvelous.

Here physical helps also are provided; indeed a vital vigor is given to the spirit that spills over into bodily health and energy. Because she is inebriated with that most precious wine which took the Apostles out of themselves when the Divine Spirit came down on them: the same, in some measure, happens to the soul which has received this gift.

...In this instance, the soul is brought by the Lord into the cellar of this excellent wine, where, carried away by this most exhilarating drink, she lives in the strength of the love of and in the energy of the fire of the Holy Spirit....In this state a soul is rarely if ever upset by any adverse event that could befall her.

33. Spiritual Exercises for December, med. 20

My Daughter, now that you have renounced your own will to live for nothing else but to do my Will, I must be installed as the only Ruler and King of your heart, I must remain in possession of, command and give direction to, all the movements of your spirit. This is so as to control and adjust it to the sphere of the Divine and to leave me the only Motor Power of your spirit and of everything that is yours.

I want nothing else but to see you on fire with the pure flame of love for me, and in this flame you will see me because this flame will, at one and the same time, set you afire and give you light to see me within you as the Life of your soul and the Motor Power of your movements. In this way you will see the love with which I have loved you from eternity and you will turn your back on created things, because your life will be in the uncreated and eternal Good. This flame will go on consuming you until you reach the point of offering yourself to me as a perfect holocaust.

This flame of the Holy Spirit which welds you to your God consumes, as by fire, every imperfection that wells forth from the worldly elements of your heart.

When every trace of earthly stain is burnt away, you will see me in the light of this same flame as Moses saw me in the burning bush, that is: your spiritual eyes will see me: your ears will hear my voice; my perfume will refresh you; and your mouth will savor me as the food that saves; and by your touch you will feel me with the delight of eternal purity which is beyond all wordly feeling.

Your food should be love and its flame that glows day and night until you are turned into fire. Your whole being should be one with this fire, since it burns you. You should yearn for this fire so that it might burn you and leave you in the ashes of a genuine humility, where you live no longer to yourself but live afire in this eternal flame which continually burns and gives light through all eternity. Thus, the soul is called to become nothing as far as created things are concerned, in the ashes produced by this divine fire, and dead to the world in everything, and to be alive only for love in love, and to burn to the point of becoming fire with the Fire until there is no difference between the two.

34. Exercise of Love for Every Day, February 26

You wish to declare that we ought to strive to arrive at the highest possible degree of charity that can be reached on earth, with the help of your divine grace....

Through the union of charity we come to possess by participation that divine perfection which is found in its essence in our Heavenly Father. There the unity of charity makes his infinite perfections to be ours to the extent that our virtuous acts are performed by God in us and by us in God.

That is what you wished to grant us to know, so that we could strive with all our energy to acquire this true charity of God and of the neighbor, from which all the Christian virtues that form a true, wholly heavenly perfection are derived: a perfection similar to that of our Divine Father who, out of the infinite charity with which he loves himself, has generated his beloved Son from all eternity, and from this Son and from himself they together have caused the Holy Spirit to proceed. From this source have come forth all the works of creation, of conservation and of redemption with the infinite mercy, and the harmony of all the virtues which are resplendent in these works, namely:

The charity of the Son resulting in the extraordinary self-abasement of coming from heaven for our salvation and submitting to so much suffering and contempt; the patience shown in bearing with the ingratitude of the sinner; the endurance and the strength and all the other virtues which this Man-God practiced with such perfection, all of them begotten of charity and brought to us. This was not only to demonstrate them to us but to cause the same charity that he had to be engendered in us, so that with our charity united to his we might arrive at the possession of all his other virtues and come to be united to the perfection of our Heavenly Father. He created us as his children in that perfection and he preserves us in being what we are.

Oh, Charity, how little have I desired you and esteemed you! How much should I not strive to acquire you, the fountain from which wells forth every virtue and perfection, to the extent of giving me possession of the supreme Good and Perfection in essence. There you make over to me the good things of my Heavenly Father and make me heir of the eternal beatitude, giving me possession of all.

Through the door of this God made Man you will enter into this perfection because in him you will be united to the Father through this divine charity.

35. The Little Garden, 9
A brief spiritual memorandum of great importance for those who truly want to make progress in the spirit.

The spiritual soul should practice three exercises on earth.

The first: to live among creatures only to help them to act well and to gain eternal salvation; otherwise not to live with them but to live in eternity away from everything created.

The second: to seek only the glory of God and the good of your neighbor in thought, word, and deed.

The third: to live only in God by means of that union with which the most holy soul of Jesus was united to the Word in God the Father and his Holy Spirit which proceeds from them both. This was the perpetual exercise of Jesus Christ, Man-God, while he was a *Wayfarer* on earth.

The soul should not come to a halt or waste time brooding over its past life, or its present, or its future, but should concentrate on this sole objective, namely, on the Unique Supreme Eternal Good, the only Beginning and the last End of all things, and on walking with pure faith, in the light of that infinitely perfect Light, at every moment of our life.

36. The Little Garden, 11
You will not moan and groan about your neighbor whenever she persecutes you, injures, or calumniates you, but you should always remind yourself of your sins and of your great deeds of ingratitude toward your Creator, and that there is no punishment or tribulation in this world, however great, that

can give satisfaction to God for a single sin. For sin merits eternal punishment; just as my Goodness is infinite so also the punishment deserved by sin is infinite.

And so be convinced always that you are lacking the light needed to grasp this truth, and consequently remain in your nothingness and there you will be sure to possess every good.

Believe in the graces you know that I give to my friends and you will participate, by benevolence, in the good things which are theirs, and it will be pleasing to me that you will thank me for them as though you had received them for yourself.

c. *Hope*

37. Degrees of Prayer II, 13 (4)

The certainty of hope that faith produces begets in the soul a most complete and sublime confidence in its dear God.

...This soul never has doubts about its God, has no fears of the arrangements which her Beloved makes; whether these be painful or pleasing to the senses, the soul never distrusts them or fears them.

All this results in an invincible strength in performing all the works to which the Divine Goodness is pleased to guide her during her exile in this world.

...Ah! How totally convinced she is that her Beloved is infinitely rich, powerful, holy, perfect. He cannot do her any injustice, cannot make a mistake, cannot lie, is not subject to instability. She knows that he specializes in doing good to and in loving the one who loves him with her whole heart.

38. Degrees of Prayer II, 11 (4)

And how can I describe the peace, the contentment, and the security that the soul enjoys in this prayer?

She reposes in a secure Refuge under these divine wings: there she hides herself in a passive giving of herself over as a gift, totally dependent on her Beloved. There she puts all her hopes; there she hides all her miseries; there she finds rest from all her crosses; there she places all her desires; there she is content in the face of every punishment, suffering, and insult received from creatures.

In this place of repose, she acts like the sheep under the care of its own shepherd, which allows itself to be milked, to be shorn, to be dipped, and to be carried on the shepherd's shoulders where he wills and as he pleases; with him the sheep is peacefully at rest.

Therefore, all fears are banished from the heart on the strength of the great security flowing over the soul.

39. Colloquies I, 6 (10)

You say to me: I should not feel that the nobility of my being is debased under the control of anything created, and you instruct me by declaring that the generosity of the upright spirit should be such that it is not demeaned by enduring the insults of the world and of creatures, and that the dislikes and the rash judgments of others should not make it unhappy.

But it should live peacefully serene in the pure act of loving, in all situations, whatever you decide, as if everything else did not exist.

40. Colloquies VII, 61 (76)

Only in the distrust of your own powers should you find the key to your real strength! Know Daughter, that I require this kind of self annihilation of you for this purpose, to give perseverance through it to my elect souls, that is, to those who, having no faith in their own powers, put all their trust in their only Good, which I am.

My goodness goes out in exact proportion to the amount of this trust that my friends have in me.

They give me all honor by such confidence, which is the root of the love they have for me. Thus it was with the woman of whom it is written in the Gospel that she said: "If I only touch the hem of his garment, I shall be made whole."

In the same way, I said to you: "If only you have confidence in me in all your concerns, you will be saved." If ever you say to me "Remember us, Lord!" everything will be adequately looked after.

Accordingly, I want you always to keep before your eyes your own weakness and your own misery and to experience occasionally how much you need me, so that you may learn to distrust yourself and to take refuge in the protection of my Divine Providence.

For my elect this confidence in me is the channel by which they acquire true strength and final perseverance.

*** Yes, no sooner have you taught me confidence in you than my spirit has clung to you as a little child clings to its mother's neck.

41. Colloquies IX, 132 (127)
Holy Father, grant me this Son, your Word, who has redeemed me and in whom are all my hopes. My soul longs for him, and all the marrow of my soul and body desire him and call for him, with sighs which are silent but which ardently yearn for him before you day and night.

Grant me him whom I love, in whom I trust, in whom I live; grant me my recompense, grant me possession of that Good who is my whole Good; grant me my Salvation, my Peace, my true and eternal Security!

d. *Chastity*

42. Rules, Purity, 6r-6v (171)
"Blessed are the clean of heart, for they shall see God" (Mt 5:8).

Those who are clean of heart know my Father because they *gaze fixedly* with affection and love on the Eternal Sun of Justice; as the eagles gaze on the sun without batting their eyelids, so there are many generous souls who gaze with love on their First Cause and last Eternal End with strength derived from love.

These are those souls who, loathing the filth and repulsiveness not only of sin itself, but of every shadow of it, never set foot on that slime, nor become, even in a small way, bogged down in the miseries of that world.

These are the children of the light who do not dwell in darkness, because bent on always having the pure intention, they keep their *gaze fixed* on the mirror of the divine perfections of their God.

It is fitting, then, that you as children of light and as white doves should not soil yourselves with the loathsome stains which can arise in the mind and in the feelings of the heart and of the body. You should keep clear of any kind of uncleanness and of anything whatsoever that could be an obstacle to your union with the Divine and to your eternal happiness.

For this purpose, keep careful guard over your senses: your eyes so that they may not look on any object that provokes concupiscence, your ears so that they may relish listening to my words and keep them in your heart and your tongue so that it may not express affection for creatures. Your sense of touch should be chaste and your heart pure so that in it may flower that Lily which is the Wisdom and Eternal Word of the Father, uncreated Light, infinite and eternal.

I am the one whom you should resemble in all these things; for during my Life I gave you outstanding examples of them.

Glory be to God forever. Amen.

43. Rules, Constitutions, 22v (172)
The sacred spouse in the Canticles praises her Beloved and says that he seeks his nourishment among the lilies, to denote the love he

has for purity. Purity is for him a robe, so to say, of fragrant flowers, which makes him shine with immaculate radiance.

Pure souls united to him, who are adorned with this excellent virtue and who keep the doors of their senses closed, are called lilies.

44. The Little Garden, 11
Daughter, see to it that your longing is always to be united with my Spirit by denying yourself everything that might not be conducive to purity.

You will perform all your actions with purity of intention for my glory alone. And just as the body breathes the air it receives to maintain the life of the body, so by breathing in my love at every moment your heart should have the life of its soul in me and take my Will as the center of its desires and satisfactions.

And in this way you will experience a transport of love in everything that happens, be it a happy or a contrary event. In trials and crosses you should be like fire that burns all the more when the wood is dry, that is, feed the flames of love with aridity, crosses, calumnies, and contempt of creatures.

Be steadfast even if you should have to lay down your life, to show fidelity to me, such as I did in laying down my life for your salvation.

45. The Little Garden, 12
Love me, me alone, with purity; and in being faithful in loving me, you will leave no room

for love of a created being. Do not nurture in your heart desires or affections which might not have been purified by my love.

46. Autobiography, 93 (185)

I was given by the Lord a light of love by which he made clear to my soul in what Divine Purity consists, and by which he wanted to espouse my soul in this life.

It seemed to me that I saw in the Heart of my Lord Jesus Christ the Three Persons in their Divine Purity; that is, the Father, the Son, and the Holy Spirit. This Purity was communicated to the three faculties of my soul on which my Spouse, Jesus, imprinted three crosses with his Precious Blood.

The first cross, signifying the Purity of God the Father, was imprinted in the memory with the Divine Omnipotence that pervades the creation of every creature, by a simple act of his Will and his infinite power, for the purposes of his Divine love.

The second Purity was communicated by the Son to the intelligence by his Word of Divine Truth where the Divine and uncreated Wisdom dwells.

The third Purity was given by the Holy Spirit to my will. And this is the infinite joy of eternal bliss — to be loved by God and to love him.

47. Colloquies II, 12 (118)

I thank you, my faithful lover, for the great love you have for me. O my beloved Spouse, I, to please you, desire to be newly dressed with an angelic and divine purity, because I know that it is this purity which is pleasing to you, my Lord.

But I see myself as a sinful mass, full of ingratitude and imperfections, and especially of that self-love which you abhor. What shall I do, my Lord?

I come to you, my safe Refuge, in order that you with your power may cause everything in me to be pure.

What can I do, I who am poor and in need of mercy and who cannot carry out even a single task without faults, and who in just one hour commit a hundred, even a thousand, infidelities.

Do thou, my Lord, apply a remedy to these evils which for my part are beyond remedy, because in the very good works that I do there is for you a loathsome uncleanness.

My King of Immaculate Purity, do thou do the needful. I rely on you alone with full confidence for this favor.

48. Colloquies III, 20 (30)

O my dearly beloved, you would not be able to hear my voice had I not beforehand touched your spirit profoundly with the kiss of Purity. By the light of my Spirit, you are purified of those stains which hamper you and, thus renewed by my love, you feel that loving touch which hastens liquefaction, issuing from my first illumination, before I effect my union with you.

The liquefaction that purifies you arises from the view which your soul has in the light of my Spirit, and thus are your repulsive stains removed and you regain the beautiful resemblance to me which you had at first.

Then the union between me and your soul is achieved; and without the purifying process that preceded I would not be able to unite myself to your soul.

49. Colloquies III, 21 (32)

I have given you possession of me in this life because of the ardent desire of your soul to be alone with me. This hunger and longing cause you to be jealous of me just as I, your Spouse and God, am most jealous of you, and cause you never to be separated from me!

My desire, Daughter, is never to find you with someone other than me, your one and only Good, nor to see you fix your thoughts on anything that creatures do, say, or think, or be anxious about their loving you, condemning you, or blaming you. For in all these things what are you looking for but the satisfaction of your own self-love? I alone am all you need in time and in eternity.

As long as you live thus jealously attached to me, the Father dwells in you well-pleased with my Divinity.

You will not live your life in yourself but I shall live in you, and in your living for me I shall live.

50. Colloquies III, 23 (34)

Listen, Daughter, if I address you by the title of my dearly beloved Spouse and by many other such titles of endearment and grandeur, if I give you those pure embraces and kisses that are so full of graces, and if I show you so many beautiful things which are as yours and in you, know that I do all these things for my Christ who is in your soul.

And when I say to you: my friend, the only beautiful, most pure spouse of my Heart, I am truly speaking to you, but it is to him that I am addressing these words, to him who is Life in you, because your person is my spouse.

In him every individual soul is my beautiful, beloved, dear spouse and each soul so united is my only dear and beautiful one: it is enough that it be caught up in this union.

*** In loving him I love you, for in espousing myself to this Spouse I espoused you: you are one in all things and all things are one in you; you are stamped as one image, one seal; you are a single imprint; you form one nature, one spouse, one love.

Hence, you are for me alone and I am for you alone; I am your Solitude and Repose; I am your sweet Company, your profound Center of peace where I accomplish that which I promised I would come to do, for the sons of men, my mansions.

*** You will receive the most delicious love of purity that goes beyond all imagining.

51. Colloquies V, 31 (47)

My spouse, I want to give you a new method of prayer different from those of the past: "My spouse, my joy has been in reclining on your heart, do thou recline your head in my Heart and rest in my bosom." Behold, my bosom is prepared for you and I shall recline my face on your neck and you will share my joy through participation in love. And that is what is called Divine Delight, which is found in the most simple performance of my Will.

*** Everything that exists, exists for this my delight and good pleasure. Thus, you will have the delight of my Delight, in every created thing: in the sun, in the moon, in the stars, in the heavens, in the earth, in the plants, in the characteristics of creatures, in current events. This delight transcends every joy of the senses, surpasses every sensuous passion. It is a Delight that is pure and divine.

And let this be your response in prayer and at work; let Delight in me be your bed, your food, your cell, your life, your spirit, your desire, your hope, your security.

52. Colloquies VI, 37 (54)

In my Divine Heart there are three acts of divine Purity that proceed from the Father, from the Son, and from the Holy Spirit.

The first Purity is given to you by the Father in his omnipotence to be enjoyed by your faculty of memory.

The second Purity comes from the Word to your faculty of intelligence: and this is engraved by the wisdom of God in your soul.

The third Purity, proceeding from the Father and the Son, is communicated to your will: and this is the divine and infinite Delight experienced in eternal bliss.

53. Colloquies VI, 42 (58)

My beloved, "with all this" you teach me how "I should comport myself" in your presence, with the candor of a child with its mother. That is, that I be pure in memory, pure in intelligence, pure in will, pure in the functioning of the senses, so that I may not be engrossed in anything which is done or said by creatures. "Teach me" to pass over, with the candor of an infant, everything in this life and renounce it voluntarily, ignoring totally every created thing, and every human judgment, whether coming from others or from myself.

54. Colloquies VIII, 78 (88)

I shall give you an instruction with an important secret which comprises in itself the beginning and the end of holiness. Be careful to act on it if you wish to free yourself from every insult of the devil, from every kind of temptation, and from every passion that rebels against my love. *It is the pure intention.*

*** Do you wish to know what soul in heaven enjoys the greatest degree of holiness? Precisely the one who in life had the most pure intention motivating her activities.

Daughter, this rightness of intention is called justice; by it the human person imitates my Divinity.

*** The greater your diligence in keeping this purity of intention, the greater will be your holiness.

My Spirit will teach you and stimulate you, in practicing this exercise, to perform sublime acts of love, and to be motivated by great purity of intention.

This should serve not only to be of profit to yourself, but in addition I tell you to explain it to every soul desirous of striving for perfection.

*** The intellect and the will of those persons who are excellently set in the way of this right and pure intention, reproduce in their spirit a copy of my Divinity.

55. Colloquies VIII, 86 (95)
In order to be able to live with everybody, be motivated by the pure intention and by charity.

*** Act as if I alone existed for you. Do not seek to satisfy the taste of your appetite or seek esteem or the love of any creature whatsoever, because all this is nothing else but you wanting to live in the heart of creatures and wanting that they live in your heart; in that way your spirit becomes demeaned, as it were, in childish games and is burdened with anxiety about its freedom and its purity of intention.

Love me more than all the things of earth; with the eye of your mind *fix your gaze* on me with purity of intention in all things — even the least.

56. Colloquies IX, 98 (104)

You had in your hands, it seemed to me, a golden key, and you locked my heart with a strong lock and placed this key in your own Divine Heart.

You then gave me to understand the meaning of this entire operation: that no creature, and still less any affection for a created thing, should gain entry into my heart, and that this key represents the pure and inviolable love that my spirit would have for you.

It seemed to me that there was engraved on that key the seal and the imprint of a Lamb, which symbolized the dominion and rule and absolute control that you had over my heart. You told me that you would never give anybody this key, thereby indicating to me how jealous you were of any other love on my part.

57. Exercise of Love for Every Day, February 10

Our Savior, in his Purity as God and Man, traces a portrait of himself in all those souls given to him by the Father, a portrait of that divine beauty in which the Father is totally pleased, and there he asks that this grace of Purity, this gift from heaven, might come to the impure and corrupt earth of our flesh.

Oh my Savior, my Lily of Purity, Unique and Beautiful, oh how many hearts are attracted by your fragrance! And your fragrance is attractive beyond all telling. If there be no purity, you have a horror of being united to an impure heart; as long as it remains unpurified by you, you do not admit it to your embrace. And since this fact is known by your faithful lovers who are enamored of such beauty, they consecrate themselves by vow to you as your chaste spouses. They are so enamored of you, O Infinite Beauty, because they are able to please you and rejoice in your Divine Purity.

Grant me, my Love, to possess this good in you, because you are my Purity most fair, and see to it that neither in a big way nor in a small way I tarnish this virtue in me.

e. *Poverty*

58. Rules, 5v–6r (169)

"He who does not renounce all that he possesses, cannot be my disciple" (Lk 14:23).

If you wish to love me and imitate me, you should carefully consider how I put value on the goods of this world and on the honors and riches of earth. From the hour of my birth until I expired on the cross, I lived a life of total poverty from childhood to my last breath. I was born in a stable, I was laid in a manger for animals, I went as a fugitive to a foreign land, enduring the worst effects of poverty.

In adulthood I procured poor food for myself by the monotonous toil of my hands in the workshop of Joseph.

In later years when I went out to preach the Word of God to the world in the face of difficulties, exhaustion, and sweat, I got support for myself and my disciples from what was proffered by devout persons. I gave my body rest by lying on the ground, for the most part under the skies, exposed to the extremes of weather like a poor beggar. Finally, I died on the wood of the cross, naked and devoid of every comfort.

That is how I esteemed the good things of this world which people love so much.

Similarly, you, my imitators, ought to have the same kind of esteem for them. Already you proposed to leave the world and all its goods for my sake. Now you should not want to possess them, to love them, to hanker after them, and to prize them, but be content to renounce them totally, and likewise to renounce everything you have a taste for and that pleases you, in regard both to the spirit and the body. You ought to deny yourself every kind of convenience and be content to be without the most necessary things so that you may take possession of my eternal riches. These are reserved for the poor in spirit who are able to sacrifice their own will and good pleasure for me. May God be glorified forever. Amen.

59. Rules, Constitutions, 21 21v-22 (170)
Holy poverty requires not only detachment from temporal goods but likewise poverty of spirit, as Our Lord says very clearly in this Rule. All affection for, desire of, and personal claims on the use of these should be severed. There should be no seeking after the satisfaction of the appetites of the senses or of the flesh.

And these souls will be the true daughters of the Most Holy Savior who not only abstain from superfluous things and from their own comforts and enjoyments, but in imitation of him rejoice in not having things that are even necessary.

60. Exercise of Love for Every Day, February 24

On this day, my Lord, give my spirit an instruction out of paradise: teach me the humble renunciation I ought to have not only of every temporal ownership of the good things of this world, but of the possession of, and the inclination toward anything that is not directed to you, O my supreme Good. In that way I will be able to live unencumbered by possession of, or inclination toward, any created thing.

O my Love, to him who asks the tunic of us you want us to give the mantle as well. By this simile you wish to make clear to me the measure of detachment and of nakedness of spirit that should characterize a Christian soul professing to be your disciple and follower. Without making any claims for herself, she should in humility spontaneously give up every right of proprietorship over herself in true poverty of spirit which is the sister of humility. She should yield to her neighbor without being contentious in any matter where she has the right in such a way that she never seeks herself in anything and gives her whole self to the One who created her out of nothing. For we must understand that we should find in this nothingness the One who is infinite being, that immense treasure which alone is the truly valuable and eternal Good.

61. Exercise of Love for Every Day, April 13

My dearly Beloved, everything beautiful, good and valuable you have created in this visible world can never satisfy, even partially, the yearnings of the human person.

...No amount of money can satisfy this appetite of the will. It can be fully satisfied and sated only by its infinite Creator God in whose image it was fashioned by you its craftsman from eternity.

Thus it is, O Word of God, my Love, in you is found the fullness of every good by the loving soul, there it finds true satiety. Nothing, neither the beauty of all the created things in this world, nor the wealth of the rich, of the kings and lords of the earth, nor the honors of the great, nor the immensity of the sea, nor all the ornaments with which you have embellished the earth and the heavens, can ever satisfy a heart capable of possessing the infinite Good.

You, my Love, tempt the soul which loves you and you ask her how her will can be totally satisfied while she lives in deprivation, and bereft of all those visible things which appeal to the senses, and while she is, by way of this total renunciation and annihilation, poor in respect of the transitory goods symbolized by money.

And in her humiliations and poverty she lies prostrate in her own heart with an infinite longing to be sated with the eternal and durable goods of the only and one supreme Good.

But she does not know how to reach you because she knows herself to be incapable of doing anything good. She sees herself to be poor because she does not possess those true riches, namely, the virtues and the good things of God alone.

And, accordingly, you, my Love, attract her, that is, you stir up in her a longing for your eternal good things. These you show this soul — in the repose she enjoys with you — to be found only in you; these good things are such that they cause her to die every hour with a desire and longing to possess you the one true, purest and most precious Good, the Word God-Man.

Those to whom you show your treasure, which are fully enclosed within you, regard it as a miracle that the body and soul can survive and not die of this great hunger of love.

f. *Obedience*

62. Rules, Obedience, 6v-7r (173-174)

"I have come down from heaven not to do my own will but the will of him who sent me....You are my friends if you do what I command you" (Jn 6:38; 15:14).

Daughters of my Heart, to teach you the perfection of this excellent virtue I came down from heaven to earth, I took the form of a servant, submitting myself to my creatures, and I embraced all the sufferings of the ignominious death of the cross.

Observe how I wanted, by my perfect obedience, to make up completely for the injury
done by disobedient man to my Heavenly
Father by his disobedience. Thus, by my obedience I gave to all creatures the norm and
example they ought to follow to honor the
precepts and commandments of their
Creator, and the way they should deny their
own will in everything in order to carry out
your Will. All this I did especially for you and
for those who wish to follow me closely by
imitating me.

And for this reason you ought promptly to
obey my commandments and those of the
Church, and the vows and obligations of
your state, as also my evangelical counsels
contained in the present Rules that have
come out of my Heart. These are the will and
prescriptions of my Heavenly Father. These
you should observe to the last jot with
promptness, joy, and simplicity.

Obey then promptly not only the words of
your superiors but the hints and the intentions
of those who represent my Person on earth, as
far as your limitations and weakness permit.
Similarly, be prompt to obey the call of the bell
which invites you to the Office of my praise so
that you may be beloved Daughters of your
Heavenly Father and that he may love you as
he has loved me. Glory be to God. Amen.

63. Rules, Constitutions, 23r (174)

In the Rule the Lord has indicated his marvelous obedience in his most perfect carrying
out of the Will of God his Eternal Father, to
the point of laying down his life: he offered

his life as a holocaust and in pure obedience willed to die the harsh death of the cross.

Hence, in imitation of him, the sisters will have an altogether special love of this virtue. United to this Divine Lover, they will renounce their own will and their own judgment, denying themselves proprietorship of everything both natural and spiritual and doing the Will of God by doing the will of the superiors who direct them.

One will only: just as the Divine Persons are only one God in the Divine Unity, so all the sisters will form a single unity in their Master, Christ Man-God.

64. Colloquies II, 7 (11)

My spouse, leave your freedom to will, or not to will, at my disposal and in my Providence. Make your will the echo of mine: if I should decide to say to you "Cross," reply willingly "Cross, yes." If I should say "Humiliations," "Contempt," echo in reply "Contempt, yes." And if I should say, "Kiss me with the kiss of tender union," answer me with the tender echo of love, "Kiss me," in such a way that you absolutely neither desire nor will anything else but the desires of my Will.

Do not seek or desire even things which are to your spiritual or temporal advantage. Thus I would have total dominion over your heart. While you are living your life indeed, I am living as though I alone were living your life and you did not live in yourself.

65. Colloquies IX, 135 (128)

My soul, Lord, has obeyed you according to

what you have said, because you, Man-God, obey the prescriptions of God your Father in me and because that is what he in his Providence decrees. My soul thus remains immobile in itself because you, Word of God, are living and you bid me to live as though I did not live.

66. Colloquies IX, 150 (137)

When I found myself in the presence of my Lord to recommend to him a matter concerning my neighbor, God my Father most clement manifested himself in spirit to my soul and said to me: "Leave it to me your Father to take care of your concerns and of yourself. I am your Father, what you want I will grant you."

All three Divine Persons showed themselves to me in spirit. God my Father received me as his daughter for ever and gave me a most richly adorned robe that covered me completely; it symbolized his Divine Will with which he wanted me to be clothed at all times as his true daughter. Then the Word, the God of love, declared me to be his spouse forever with endearing words of love, and he gave me a most beautiful ring and a little cross of gold studded with most precious stones and diamonds so dazzling and beautiful that they defy description. It was the same with the ring: a diamond with three precious stones at its three corners to set it off in a way that the whole seemed to form a single stone: this symbolized the fidelity due to him in all my activities until death. The cross had five huge diamonds and the gold sparkled with resplendent rays: and these rays enveloped certain ruby stones which blazed like a fire. The Holy Spirit was the one who decorated me and did all these things.

This very beautiful cross had five stones and these symbolized the five degrees of abasement of the Word, the Spouse of God: one was his own self-annihilation, the second his being insulted, the third the contempt shown him, the fourth his hidden condition, the fifth the abandonment he endured. The gold was the Divine Love with which he loved the cross. And those little rubies that sparkled in the cross were the graces, the merits, and the value of the humiliations with which he decorates the souls in question.

Then the Divine Lover decorated my soul with these his presents as being his beloved spouse, signifying that he was clothing my soul with his virtues. He then took his Divine Heart into his hands with great and tender love...and said to my soul: "Receive this my heart to love me with my own love for ever."

67. Degrees of Prayer IV, 31 (12)
Jesus, as man, cast off the garment of his own liking and good pleasure and will and gave preference to wearing the garment of his Father's Will.

To this he adds that he will dress himself again with this garment (of his Father's Will) through the action of his beloved spouse when she, loving soul, through her imitation of him, consecrates to him her wishes and desires. Thus she, together with Jesus, offers these to the Divine Father by living not for her own preference or desire, but solely to be pleasing to God.

...The good pleasure of God was his robe, the same with which he seeks to have his spouse enrobed. He wants that to be his robe because he does not wish to appear in any other robe but that of the Will of God. For this purpose he cast off the garment of his own self-will, that is, he rejected every human wish or impulse by making it subservient to the Will of God. He rejected every movement of self-will by sacrificing his own will to the Will of his Father. And so he dressed up the totality of human nature, which his human nature represented, with the robe of the divine good pleasure and holy Will, including all the lovers who live in him by love.

Hence, the soul to whom God has granted the grace to understand that to be united to the life of Jesus is the divine good pleasure...becomes a solid rock. Neither the cross nor the tempest nor tribulations can move it from its center. This soul would much rather be cut to pieces by all creatures than act on a single impulse of self-will in opposition to the Divine Will and good pleasure.

Accordingly, she unflinchingly endures everything disposed by the Divine Will. She does more than simply suffer, she embraces with very great peace all the assaults of the devil and all the revolts of her own nature. As for all the harsh and unpleasant experiences of the senses which assail her, she is so bent on denying them and doing them to death that they are suppressed and killed off in her in the same instant. Not only does she not allow (uncharitable) words to reach her lips but she does not give them access even to her heart.

68. Spiritual Exercises for December, med. 19

Jesus, paradise of souls on earth united to the Divine Will. Daughter, by the union achieved with the Divine Word in the sacrament of the Eucharist your will should be so transformed into that of my Son that you ought not exercise any act except that which is one with the Will of your God. This means that the phrase "The Will of God" is tantamount to your will, and that there is nothing in your will other than the Will of God. Both will the same thing and reject the same thing, you are one with him in love and one with him in the same Spirit. Consequently, everything my Divine Providence has ordained for you, both adverse and favorable, should be loved and accepted by you with love while you repose like a babe committing itself to the care of its mother and sleeping peacefully and resting without any worry, preoccupation, or care about itself and its interests.

There, Daughter, is the paradise of souls wayfaring on earth united by love to my Beloved Son. There he achieves the union of all the souls who are mine with the Deity, and this in so perfect a way that the soul comes to the point of willing with the Will of God himself.

It is able to deny itself and renounce any act not in conformity with my Divine Will and continually put to death every movement of self-will.

In this matter you should be faithful and live by the divine life of your God while you are still a wayfarer on earth. Because by ceasing to be led by your own will in everything, and by following whatever I should arrange for you, you will enjoy an anticipated Paradise. For by accepting me and all that I ordain and by submitting yourself with all your will and judgment, you will be granted to see my well-ordered scheme of things even down to the changes in the seasons. You will not be disturbed by sufferings and crosses. Nor will the miseries of human life cause you pain, because in being united by love to my Son you will enjoy a life of untroubled peace.

As my Son, during the sufferings of the cross, was all the time participating in the glory he enjoyed through the union of his soul with the Divinity, so you, by leaving behind every created being and becoming immersed in him and united to him by love, will, even here on earth, always remain in the glory he experiences in the very happy moments of my eternity. And there, the embraces of your Mother will be very sweet; you will be in a safe harbor protected from every enemy.

And in this context remember the words of my Son — whoever receives one of these little ones receives me, and their angels always gaze on my face because my light of truth shines out from their souls even while they are still on earth.

g. *Liturgy*

69. Autobiography, 66 (125)
Of all other times of her life the most pre-

cious were the sacramental communions....At Holy Communion the Lord caused her to feel herself transformed into Jesus. Then in a divine light all the virtues of the holy Life of our Lord Jesus Christ were stamped upon her and filled her soul with the utmost joy.

One morning at Holy Communion the phrase recited at the Creed of the Mass, *"consubstantial with the Father,"* was pronounced in the center of her soul in a way that filled and perfumed her soul with good things as though it were suffused with balsam. There together were all the virtues that rose like incense from the Word of God made Man, and her soul understood that these virtues should regulate all the actions of her life and of the lives of all the just.

...On another morning at Holy Communion...the soul in question was surprised by an extraordinary recollection...while carried beyond every created object: a fountain of grace and a very voluminous river surged up in the Word and flowed forth from the Word containing all the perfections and virtues he showered on her.

Then the Lord Jesus Christ made her a present of his Divine Heart. He gave it to her in exchange for her own with infinite love...and gave her at the same time his most holy Life, with unbreakable promises of uniting her to himself eternally in faith, hope, and love. It seemed to her that the Holy Spirit took her will and united it to, and transformed it into, the Will of God. In this way it seemed that her soul, from that moment, was raised to a new life.

70. Colloquies II, 13 (19)

When you receive me sacramentally, have the will to receive the baptismal stole in my Divine Heart and in my Blood. And it is certain that every time you enter into me in a union of love, you will go out only in a beautiful and pure condition.

71. Colloquies II, 16 (24)

If an evil-minded creature united with the devil can do such an evil thing, what, do you think, can a creature of good will united with love of pure charity to my Divine Heart, which has absolute sovereignty over it, not do?

Now I will teach you what to do to bind to my Heart the sinners who have been recommended to you. When you receive me in the Most Holy Sacrament of the Eucharist, unite, in an irrevocable gift, your will and your whole self and offer it for all time to my Heart, together with the will of all the martyrs with their blood united to my Precious Blood, as well as with the heart of all those who love me and have loved me. With the heart of my Mother and "with" the hearts of obstinate sinners bind them in my Heart and wash them with my Blood and present them thus to my Father and entreat him for the sake of my Heart to make this bond unbreakable for you. I assure you that, for my part, I will never deprive you of it, neither you nor any of those who do it with the total affection of their heart.

72. Colloquies IX, 147 (135)

(The soul) — This morning I went to Holy

Communion and you changed me into yourself, because I entered into the Humanity of your Divine Word and began to sacrifice myself to the Father for all mankind, something I have never experienced in the past.

(The Lord) — From the Offertory of the Mass began my offering of myself to my Father in satisfaction for all the sins of the world: I sacrificed my will to his Divine Will in a perfect sacrifice as in the Garden (of Olives), and in the sacrifice I endured all the actions of my Passion to my last breath on the cross, to the consummation of my sacrifice.

I experienced all the precious and divine acts which my soul had accomplished most perfectly, and also the ineffable glorification the enjoyment of which my soul has now, by my Passion, merited in every sacrifice which is celebrated in my Church.

And I still get relish from all the graces and merits which all the souls of the faithful receive through my Passion: all of them are glorified in my Humanity — in my Humanity alone united to the Word.

No created mind or intellect can be capable of this total glorification: only my Divinity can grasp the quantity and the quality of these benefits.

73. Colloquies IX, 148 (136)

One morning at Mass you, my dearest Love, called my soul, as is your wont into an interior and intimate union with you in Holy Communion.

...You bade me sacrifice myself in this union with you to your Divine Father during the Mass. We were joined together to the sacrifice and perfect holocaust of the cross — in this way while the Divine Word, God-Man, was offering himself as victim for all the sins of the world, I also became similarly sacrificed to your Divine Father and, united with you, purified of all the stains of my past sins — both of the punishment and of the guilt — made satisfaction to the Divine Justice on the strength of my union with you. You made total satisfaction for me, and you paid all my debts for me: not only that, but you clothed me with your own justice and innocence and adorned me with your divine virtues.

...You explain to me that every person who, in the sacrifice of the Holy Mass, has, with humble sentiments of affection, the will to unite its spirit with your well-beloved Son and offers all its faculties in union with the perfect holocaust of your Divine Word and sacrifices itself with him who is the Life of all persons living in God, such a soul will become cleansed of all its sins: what is more, insofar as it makes this offering of self together with the offering of the Immaculate Lamb, it will be able to satisfy for the sins of its neighbors and for the souls in purgatory.

Inasmuch as Jesus continues to sacrifice himself in God, the person united to him remains in a sacrificed state: dying to its own faculties and to the bodily senses with all their animal impulses, it causes to live in itself only the Word of God sacrificed and dead for mankind.

By being united wholeheartedly with Jesus, we will have the will to be sacrificed in Jesus to the Divine Father and to make satisfaction for the sins of all our neighbors and to cooperate with Jesus in the work of Redemption and thus give to him who is our only Good the love he deserves.

74. Spiritual Exercises for December, med. 18
I live, now not I, but Christ lives in me
in the Most Holy Sacrament of the Altar.

Beloved Daughter, remember what the Divine Word, God-Man, said, namely that he would be with you to the end of the world because he would be the food and nourishment of human beings, indeed he would be their life in the Most Holy Sacrament of the Eucharist.

O prodigious marvel of omnipotence and mercy by which the human person lives the life of God and becomes transformed into and identified with its God — to the extent that God might be called a human and a human being called God.

In this instance my mercy has not been able to go further in giving, because no greater gift can be given; and my omnipotence could not accomplish anything greater than the giving of my own Divine dear Son.

At this point hold yourself still in admiration as you contemplate the countless good things you have received.

First of all, there are the merits and all the virtues practiced by the God-Man when on his pilgrim way; all these are transformed into your soul and become yours by your union with him; all your feelings and passions become sanctified by him and transformed into his feelings and your body transformed into his; and by virtue of the hypostatic union of the body and soul of the Word with the Divinity, you gain entry to God through love and become transformed into the Blessed Trinity. To the Blessed Trinity God unites you in a way that God lives in a human person and a human person lives in God with the life itself of God.

And this Man-God has poured out all his Blood to make satisfaction to my Justice in order to bring about this union. Accordingly, he instituted this sacrament immediately before his Passion at the cost of his Blood poured out for the benefit of all. For them he would thus become their drink, their nourishment, their life and substance — all the while his Divine Body and Blood remained inseparably united to the Word.

Behold then where the salvation of the just lies, behold the source where they receive all the lights and knowledge of the eternal truths. There they are filled to full measure and overflowing from the torrent of love where they become immersed in God and made able to produce the most abundant fruits of every virtue, especially love for the neighbor, because this sacrament is love. There they receive the Holy Spirit with all his gifts because they are transformed into God by my Beloved Son. You see now, Daughter, what dignity this sacrament gives you, and how my great mercy is without bounds: there has been no restraint in my giving. Hence, your whole life should be a continual preparation for and thanksgiving to, my mercy.

75. Exercise of Love for Every Day, March 23

You, O Word of God, live in me, you dwell in my heart. God the Father says: "Behold my Beloved Son! To my Heart, to my Word, who lives in my bosom, is given the power to give life: life in faith, life in grace, life in love."

He who is my whole Good gives himself to me sacramentally in a morsel of bread. There I receive the gift of pure faith; there my innumerable ailments receive healing and all the members of my body impaired by the mass of my iniquities are strengthened. And through you, Word of God and my Word, I have received your Holy Spirit, who dwells in me and gives me life in God, life of grace and love, life of the Spirit breathed into me by you.

Love of my heart, how can I thank you! The ears of my spirit, melting with love, hear these words most sweet from you, Word of God: "Go, your son doth live," because you, God, live in the human person; in my life the Son of the Eternal Father is living, having come down into my heart to give new life to my flesh.

God-Man, in your immense charity, you have glorified me, and through you I have received the great gift of pure and unsullied faith behind the veil of the Holy of Holies.

God speaks to the soul and discloses to her his most intimate and sublime secrets, communicating them to the ear, the taste, and the touch of her soul.

76. Exercise of Love for Every Day, 178

Lily of infinite Purity, Word, God-Man, in this unleavened and pure bread of your Immaculate Flesh, my soul is transformed into you. O how I am fed with your love as I nourish myself on your Flesh, the unleavened Bread of Life.

Oh my Love, I lose myself in the vast ocean of your immense love. O Bread of supersubstantial and divine sincerity and truth, you, by your Purity, transform me into the living God, and by your Purity, convert my stained flesh into the purity of your Immaculate Flesh. Not only that, but you nurture my soul with your life of purity, and from all the wheat grains, as it were, of faithful souls you knead together a single bread baked by the fire of your divine charity in your Humanity. This bread you feed to your Word and to all three Divine Persons in you. You make me the bread of God and I, through union of love, live the life of my God through you who are eternal life. And so you are right to cry out in the words of the Holy Spirit: "Dearly beloved, eat, drink, and be inebriated."

The reception of your Flesh means that I am treated to all the viands that taste of God; the reception of your Blood means that I am given sufficient to be inebriated, because this Blood was the abundant medicine that cured all my wounds and the bath which washed me clean. In the Most Holy Sacrament this Blood is served around newly again, spiritually, in our souls by your divine charity.

Now that your sacred Humanity, united to the Word of God, has been glorified — this incorruptible glorified Flesh! It gives me such a risen life in God that it transforms me into the eternal life of God, as I await the dawning of that new day, which will make me blessed for all eternity. And you want me to be inebriated with that glorified precious Blood of yours!

Yes, my Love, I yearn to drink it to the point where my soul becomes inebriated with your divine love and all my bodily senses emptied in such a way that I may no longer be carried away by myself or by my flesh or by creatures, but inebriated by your love, I may consume you, O Word, God-Man, my only Life and my Eternal Substance!

...Yes, just as you created me in your own image and likeness, so you wished to receive me anew into yourself in the Most Holy Sacrament of the Altar, and you enabled me to nourish myself with yourself. You would have my food be "milk and honey," suckled from two breasts in this sacrament: the milk being the merits of your Humanity, already made mine, so that my life might be nursed and nourished with your virtues and your example during my present life; the honey being that most delicious food of all for me to taste, that is, my God in the honeycomb of the God-Man. For you would give me the living God as my unsurpassable delight. And you, my Love, nourish yourself in my heart with yourself, with your Love, and you make me also your food. God nourishes himself with Jesus, and I am the food of Jesus; Jesus is my eternal food of life. He is at once my Sheepfold and my Shepherd. The Shepherd eats the Lamb because he is clothed with our wool, and we his flock feed on him by way of the milk of his love.

77. The Little Garden, 9

If you have received me or are about to receive me in the Most Holy Sacrament of the Altar, plunge into the great depths of grace and gifts I have given to humans and ensure that you become wholly changed into my Life through love, and be annihilated and become dead to yourself and to all the creatures of this world. And throughout the whole day, busy yourself in giving infinite thanks and praise to my Father-God of goodness, of wisdom, and of divine charity toward the human race; to my God who has such an immense treasure house of riches so great that I alone am able to fathom their extent.

78. Autobiography, 39 (92)

My soul was so strongly drawn to you, my Love, that in the praying of the Divine Office my spirit was transported beyond myself both sweetly and irresistibly by you, O loving Word of God. Scarcely had I begun its recitation than I became immobilized and unable to continue. This was due to the intimations hidden in the Psalms: in a flash these were clearly disclosed to my soul and my heart was pierced with a dart of your Divine Love.

79. The Little Garden, 12

When you are in choir for Lauds, join that praise of yours to the Lauds (= Praises) which I, while I was *Wayfarer* on earth, offered to God my Father, and live as though I, not you, lived in yourself. Thus, all the graces, gifts, and spiritual consolations which you receive from my Love, receive them not in yourself but in me.

h. *Prayer*

80. Rules, Prayer 8v-9r (185-186)
"You must pray always and not cease to pray" (Lk 21:36).

It is necessary that people pray all the time, without any intermission so as to both free themselves from sin and to conquer their enemies. Prayer also brings a person that happiness which arises from the union of the soul with my Divinity.

Speaking of this union, the Holy Gospels say that we, the Father and the Holy Spirit and I shall make our dwelling place in a heart which is single-minded and trusting, one which only lives contemplating and loving me alone, swimming along, as it were, in the infinite stream of my eternal sweetness and my divine goodness.

Thus, if you wish to imitate me, remember that my whole life was prayer. This was the continual exercise of my Humanity: to love the Father with the same love with which he loved me.

Frequently seek out secluded places and keep nocturnal vigil on the solitary mountain tops and in that way intercede for the divine mercy for souls which I have redeemed.

In a very special way imitate me in making your own that prayer, which I offered in the

Garden of Olives before my Passion and Death on the Cross, praying in a most perfect manner the best prayer of all, placing my whole spirit in my Father's hands! This is, indeed, the most perfect prayer that a soul can make if it wishes to give me pleasure.

Therefore, pray always and at all times if you wish to acquire purity of heart. To this end you must love solitude! In everything you do, pray with humility and simplicity. Unite yourself in a union with your God who is the goal and fulfillment of all the happiness you seek. May God be eternally glorified. Amen.

81. Rules, Constitutions, 26r-27r (186-187)

Prayer and the presence of God are the very life of a religious and spiritual soul — something so strongly insisted on by the Lord himself in this Rule.

He himself has given us the example of this in the Holy Gospel where it is said that throughout the thirty years of his life before he began his preaching, he lived a hidden life in silence and in an admirable state of recollection. But in addition to this, during his three tiring years of preaching, he often went off at night into the secluded mountains and spent the night hours of repose in continual prayer in the midst of all the weakness and fatigue of his blessed tired body. This continual exercise of prayer was the food of his most Holy Soul. That is why he persistently taught this virtue of prayer in such an effective way.

...About the practice of the Presence of God that must be continually carried out each hour of the day (this is to be done) by performing all the actions of the day — as far as this is possible — in the Divine Presence within you own heart with repeated and frequent acts of love...curtailing all useless imaginations and being careful not to give the senses any useless and harmful diversions.

These acts toward God, made as frequently as possible, should center on some points of the morning meditation or on the life of our Lord Jesus Christ as the Rule itself prescribes for the various hours of the day, preserving your companionship with the Lord in the way most agreeable to him. This latter way of praying would be most useful and most in conformity with the spirit of the Rule.

82. The Little Garden, 9
In the early morning hour, as soon as you awake from sleep, focus your spirit totally on me, your Creator, and steer clear of any kind of discourse or idle speech and guard the cell of your heart in which I rest with great jealousy and diligence; try to be retired and solitary insofar as holy Obedience allows. Don't leave me all by myself in your heart!

Indeed, my Divine Heart should be your cell. There pray to my Heavenly Father continually with pure faith and love. Since I am in your heart and you are in mine, it is there, in my Divine Light, that you will recognize all your shortcomings and defects.

83. Autobiography, 11 (60)
One day the Lord called her by means of an interior voice and said to her: "Look at the material sun and see how it lights up every-

thing and gives warmth and makes the plants of this earth grow so that they produce flowers and fruits and see how it brings happiness to the world with its brightness. See how it shines everywhere, and only those who shut their windows are unwilling to receive its light and remained deprived of that light through their own fault simply because they don't want to look upon its splendor.

This sun which you see in the visible world was created as an image, a symbol of the Divine Son who illumines the interior world of the soul with his Divinity: these are the effects that my Divine Presence produces in the souls which I created. Now you, by means of the material sun which always shines, will be reminded of my divine perfections and shall behold how, with the warmth of my Spirit, I make the plants of the virtues grow in your soul, and these in turn produce the flowers and fruits of eternal life. I make light by illuminating the intellect and setting the will on fire in my divine love. In my divine warmth I dry up those evil humors which produce the disordinate passions and I destroy the soul's imperfections for those who open their eyes and look upon me and make my divine splendor enter within them, opening as it were the windows of their soul, that is, those who do not close off my light with sin. Consequently, when you behold the material sun, you will recall all I have told you and this will be a continual prayer."

84. Autobiography, 40 (93)

Above all the other teachings you spoke to me of the love of purity from which I grasped the primary importance of your Divine Presence in the spiritual life, that is, of thinking of you alone, longing for you alone, loving only you, and of not seeking or desiring anything other than yourself, the only treasure of the soul and I understand that by doing this, one is cleansed of one's bad habits and of the suggestions of the devil.

And it is in your Divine Light that the soul sees and recognizes its own dark spots and then receives from your divine perfections the garment of the holy virtues; and how many times you, my Love, spoke these most sweet words to my heart: You are mine alone and I am yours alone, do not leave me all alone in your heart.

There just was not enough time for me to live in such a secluded way or to remain in my cell or in choir or any other secluded and solitary spot in the monastery or for listening to your most sweet teachings.

85. Colloquies IV, 27 (40)
Just how much a bird leaves the earth to fly up in the air, and just how much it continues to fly higher and higher — that is the measure of how much it will enter the purer air of the heavens and find more security, since it is only in the heights that it is safe from the hunters.

And that is the way it is with the Christian soul: it is more secure and free from every predator when by its contemplation it flies unto the heights and the purer air which exists in the heaven of my Divinity.

Rise up, therefore, as high as you can, into the tranquillity of this air, where, in loving silence, fullness, and security, you shall experience a most sweet, gentle, and pure breathing.

...Those who are truly free, enjoy an uninter-rupted happiness, a joyful liberty, and a supreme peace of heart, and the most fortunate of all are those who have stronger wings so they can fly on high. The one who knows how to lift up these wings from the nothingness of all the trifling things and from the valueless-ness in the self, will rise up on high toward him who is the Infinite All of every good.

86. Colloquies VI, 47 (63)

My Daughter, do not be afraid. My Spirit which rests in the just soul, as on its own throne, is never quiet.

Since your soul is an image of my substance, what then are you in your spirit, in your being, if not a living image, a living reprint of me, yet dependent on my Being?

Fear, then, if you can! My Spirit is one and it produces all the goods that exist in every creat-ed spirit; the just person is a seat of my Divinity. It is "my Spirit" which breathes, moves, ordains, and operates in the soul and that is why you make no mistakes in terms of what is good....It produces clarity in the intel-lect, security in the will, and makes your works fruitful. And all this happens in such a way that the Spirit is like the soul of your own soul and makes it fly after and pursue the good.

87. Colloquies IX, 99 (104)

Silence is good for me. It is sufficient that I talk to you. I feel nothing can prevent or hold me back from this and you have praised and blessed this language of my heart as you made clear yes-terday when you said: "Friend of my heart, what joy and pleasure that you speak to me all the time and I always listen to you. I bless your insistent supplications which you make for your own self as well as for your neighbors."

From this statement, O God of my heart, I now well know and understand that my soul, your spouse, not only receives and rests in the sweet communications which you have with her, but that you likewise are pleased and happy that this soul lifts her voice unceasingly to you with its acts and its affections so as to seek your mercy for herself and her neighbors.

You tell me that you are happy that I rest in the sleep of your love but that you are likewise very pleased when at other times my spirit prayers will all kinds of prayer such as petition, impetration and satisfaction, thanksgiving, asking, and also with act of either vocal or mental prayer of praise, sorrow, hope, confidence, faith, and love.

Therefore, you arouse in me all these different acts, either in the heart or vocally, or rather let us say that they are set in motion by the affections of your very own love. You tell me that it pleases you when the whole person, both interior and exterior, comes to you to pray with all its affections and all its senses. And so that I may carry out all of this, you promise and actuate within me all these different ways of prayer. O that my spirit may always cry out with an infinite clamor in your presence, for you are my God!

88. Degrees of Prayer II, 12 (4)
In just one single loving glance of God one sees not only oneself but all the miseries of

one's neighbors, as well as every wish and grace that one desires.

The soul stands in the presence of its Delight. And with that one glance of love, all its needs are made clear. And this spiritual sight of the soul brings happiness not only because the soul sees but also because it is being looked upon by its Delight substantially and in a friendly and merciful way.

This is not praying (in the sense of simply repeating words), but rather a mutual exchange of being, a handing over of the heart.

From this, the spouse receives at this point all the goods of its beloved God and therefore is now granted not only all these graces which she asked for but, in addition, all her other desires. The result of this is a marvelous certitude that everything has surely been granted!

89. Degrees of Prayer XVI, 133 (50)

Prayer of petition is that by which the Lord is pleased to be asked for certain needs of the soul espoused to him or for the benefit of one's neighbor. This prayer may take various forms: it can be prompted by God himself; it can also be aroused by the needs of the soul itself, or perhaps it is stirred up by charity for one's neighbor and this, out of love for God. In any case, however, it is always God who moves one to this prayer.

This type of prayer is a form of charity which God pours into the soul for needs of the Church or for the general public. It is also for sinners or the souls in purgatory or for the benefit and perfection of good souls — all this as it pleases the Lord.

God is accustomed to give the soul an interior urge, built on confidence in God so that sometimes the soul spends entire days at prayer loving God. By just one interior glance of the soul, it shows its Lord what it desires of him, animated as it is by a filial and secure trust in God. At this point, it is God himself who is moving the soul, desirous as he is of pouring out his mercies on his creatures. And the soul, on its part, feels a security at having, in its hands, that for which it was longing and praying.

On the contrary, there are times when the soul wishes to pray for a certain thing and does all it can for this purpose but feels an interior refusal and then makes an effort to pray to the Lord. But many times it happens that, despite all its diligence, it goes to pray and can scarcely recall what it wanted to speak to and pray to the Lord about!

This is a sign that for the time being, the Lord is not pleased to hear about that which the soul wants and perhaps he wishes some greater good for the soul and for his glory.

i. *Recollection*

90. Rules, Recollection, 8r-8v (182-183)

"I will lead her into solitude and speak to her heart" (Hos 2:14).

"When you pray, do not multiply your words like the pagans; they think that they will be heard because of their sheer multiplication of words" (Mt 6:7).

A person's heart is God's throne! The heart is that secret room in which the Heavenly

Father keeps his divine treasures so they cannot be stolen by thieves. He asks of you not only a door, but he wishes that it be securely closed.

Wherefore, in the Canticle of Canticles, Wisdom says to the soul-spouse that she unlock the door of her heart because he wants to enter. This is why my faithful spouse keeps the door of her senses closed so that no thief can enter, indeed, so that no others might enter therein except her legitimate Spouse, who will let her first of all experience his voice calling to his spouse to willingly open the door to him.

That's the way it is with my faithful souls who keep the doors of their senses closed to every created object.

Therefore, you ought to observe a continuous recollection and silence of mind and heart so that you can enjoy my true peace. This is what I observed and put into practice for thirty years of my life, never opening my mouth except to give glory to my Father and to save souls.

In this way I showed the value and the high regard which I had for the hidden life and for silence since these are useful and necessary for the soul, both in terms of acquiring my virtue and gifts and of preserving the gifts, as also for hearing the messages of my Divine Wisdom which instruct the soul in secret and in the solitude of the hearts of those who love me. For this purpose, make sure you watch over the retreat times and the times of silence prescribed in these Rules in all the times and places assigned by loving to dwell in the quiet cell of your heart.

Thus, I shall find you alone with me and your will be able to participate in my divine sweetnesses. May God be eternally glorified. Amen.

91. Rules, Constitutions, 25r-26r (183-184)

The good order of Religious Houses depends on silence; and the whole of religious observance depends on the exact observance of silence.

It is equally important that each and every religious observes silence most zealously, since this is the only means to carry out the practice of prayer and of the presence of God and the door that leads the soul into true interior recollection.

...However, perfect silence consists in mortifying useless talk and fantasies which happen when one willingly talks about useless and harmful thoughts, for example, to have any communication with the devil and with temptations against the faith, scruples, passions and similar things, and perhaps also with disobedience to those who guide them who have already forbidden such voluntary thoughts or words about such material.

These things are very harmful to the soul because they shut the door on the Lord's lights and graces, leaving the soul in darkness, obtuseness, coldness, and incapable of that perfect silence and clarity of intellect and of that light in the heart which is so necessary for the good disposition of mental prayer and for the holy meditations on the life and death of the Lord, which the Rule prescribes and wants practiced at all hours of the day.

Thus, one may conclude that exterior silence of the tongue is not sufficient for peace of heart.

92. Colloquies IX, 89 (97)

As an enclosure for love's pure glance, continual silence is a necessity. Be quiet in your mind, heart, and tongue when you speak about yourself, either in praise or blame or disdain or exaggeration or humiliation. Remain silent in regard to the opinions of other people whether they are favorable or unfavorable! Be quiet! Be quiet in terms of your gifts, graces, and lights; remain silent in the changes and variations of the events of this life. Don't go out of your way to explain your blessings or your sufferings: let all things be submerged in your Purity. Have no desire to justify yourself in anything, neither with your superiors nor with your equals.

From this hour on, let your life be one of pure love, that is, your Spouse, my Word: carefulness about silence, and if you must speak in your encounters with others, let it be in the sweetness and tranquillity of my Word; before saying anything dip your tongue in the wisdom of my Divine Word....Likewise, when you are revealing something that pertains to your soul, if and when this is necessary, let the language of Purity prevent any mistaken enigmatic approach.

Consecrate your pure love to silence! Immerse all that happens to you within the circle of pure love by remaining silent, whether you suffer spiritual pains and interior trials or bodily sufferings or pains, weakness, dullness, barrenness, or tediousness of the senses — put aside every act of the senses in favor of the immaterial actions of the Spirit.

93. Degrees of Prayer XII, 97 (38)

He placed the *Sun* of his Divinity within the human person so that the person might always walk along the right ways in the light of his Divine Presence. And this Light surrounds the soul and warms it at all times and in every place so that it might produce the fruits of the virtues.

He also created the moon which gives its own light in the night of this world, that is to say the Sacred Humanity of his Divine Word as a guide which leads a person through the dark night of this world to eternal life.

He also placed the stars in the firmament, and these are all the merits of Jesus Christ, our Savior. These merits adorn our souls like jewels that shine like stars in the firmament of our souls.

94. The Little Garden, 10

You shall be diligent in your withdrawal at the hour of silence and observe the silence exactly unless charity or obedience require otherwise. And at that time, gather all things into your soul's center in a spirit of abandonment and self-forgetfulness and thus you shall dwell within my Divine Heart, attentive to that which I shall teach you with my Divine Light.

And at this time you shall remember those three dark hours during which I hung on the cross totally surrounded by the pains and sorrows of death, laying down my life for your salvation and that of all creatures.

And you shall remain there under the cross remembering the blood which I offered to my Divine Father for sinners.

l. *Conversion and Penance*

95. Rules, Mortification, 7v-8r (179-180)

"Whoever hates his life in this world preserves it for eternal life" (Jn 12:25).

Mortification of the senses of the human person is something for his benefit and is the very life of the soul, for it is by sin that a person degrades the nobility of the soul and subjects it to the consequences of his animal appetites.

I came into the world to teach you how to subject the fleshly appetites to reason and to justice, placing you instead in a slavery to my Humanity.

I took upon myself all that was bitter and the most difficult kind of mortification which no other person in the world could ever be able to take up as is apparent in the fact that I suffered poverty, hunger, thirst, nocturnal vigils, travels, tiredness, betrayal, vituperation, abandonment, contradiction, spit, buffoonery, blows, false witness, crowns, nails, gall and vinegar, the cross, abandonment, curses, blasphemies. And finally I gave up my spirit on a cruel gallows without any comfort or solace.

From the very hours of my birth until I breathed my last breath on the Cross, my life was a constant dying to the animal life of sinful man, doing penance in my Humanity for sinful man.

And so now you live in my sanctified flesh which was mortified for you and you live united to this my Body, as my very own members, like branches on the vine.

And to be united to me it is necessary that you embrace an authentic mortification of all your senses, your inclinations, bad habits, or inordinate movements, renouncing all your own likings, pleasures, and appetites. You will do this by loving vigils, fasts, abstinence, and mortification of the flesh, not looking for any satisfaction in food, sleep, or clothing or in anything else that might feed your appetite.

Consequently, the spirit, freed from these impediments, is lifted on high to its own proper sphere in order to be united to my Divinity. May God be eternally glorified. Amen.

96. Rules, Constitutions, 24v (180-181)

There is no need to explain how necessary it is for every religious to mortify herself, both in the faculties of the soul as well as in the realm of the senses, since what the Lord puts before our eyes when one considers the Rule of his most holy life is sufficient proof. There he tells of his sufferings and his most sad death on the cross, and in that life one be-holds a most admirable mortification both on the part of his soul as well as in the senses of his body.

Most of all, therefore, those religious whose Institute has no other goal than the imitation of his most Holy Life, are bound to this death of the senses in everything, because it is impossible to attain the state of perfection of his most Holy Life without this death-to-self.

Therefore, they must be dead to their own self-will and thoroughly mortified in their own judgment: and this kind of mortification is the most important and necessary.

...But above all, let them be truly attentive to the interior mortification of their passions and their senses, as also of their own judgment and will, since this is most necessary for the acquisition of Christian perfection and for union with the true imitation of Jesus and for their eternal salvation.

97. Autobiography, 62 (120)

There arose in me a desire to love and to suffer for the sake of him who loved me, however, I did not understand well the penance which the Lord desired of me; I did not know anything except bodily penance and mortification.

However, I later understood the Lord wanted a spiritual mortification in addition to this bodily penance but was not aware of this at the moment nor was I now capable of anything other than the Lord let me understand about this death-to-oneself.

98. Colloquies II, 10 (15)

My spouse, this is what I want from you; and it is that which I look for in all of my chosen souls, namely, that they dedicate themselves to getting rid of the subtle movements of self-love that are continually coming alive in the earth of one's heart.

Oh, if only the souls who truly desire me would understand how diligent they must be in examining from which spirit the motions of their hearts are proceeding! They would know with the light of truth it is only self-love that always contradicts my Love.

My Daughter, watch over your heart so that you may purify both your interior and exterior movements so that all your works may be legitimate children of my Love. Let your desires — all of them — "be only desires" of giving me pleasure; and your thoughts and words only for my glory.

Keep your eyes always focused on the impulse of the Purity of love without any fear or human respect in all that you do for yourself or for your neighbor. And know that in doing this, your operations will be really as if I and not you were operating; in this way they will have great value in my sight.

99. Degrees of Prayer XIII, 111 (43)

The devil, filled with diffidence and fears, goes around breathing out his poison so that he can put fear and diffidence within you. However, He who lives within you drives him away and gives him no room to stay and molest you. The soul itself does not act at all except to show the Lord who is within what is happening, accusing the enemy before the Lord and, having done this, it remains secure in its Lord.

It is necessary to point out here that one should pay no attention at all to such insults but should just ignore them as if they never took place. One should try not to feel such things because if you begin to be afraid, then the enemy gains the advantage for he will return again to upsetting and disturbing your peace once more. This happens in proportion to your fear.

You must put aside you own natural capacity and empty out the senses without receiving any of those evil impressions, not even examining them nor trying to understand the devil's subtleties and diabolic suggestions, just as our Lord Jesus Christ did when in the desert the devil, knowing he was hungry, presented Jesus with the stones he wanted the Lord to change into bread.

100. Spiritual Exercises for December, med. 5

My little Daughter, it is most necessary that you understand the greater benefit which a pilgrim soul experiences who lives in the world and dies in the state of grace and is saved by my mercy, namely, that supreme and greatest blessing which consists in having all its sins forgiven.

Reflect on your own self and count all the love that you have received from the first days of the use of reason even up to now and see if you can enumerate the great, innumerable number of your sins, defects, and imperfections, many of which were committed out of malice and many others out of ignorance of your early years as a child, and still others committed because of your lack of control of your passions and your fragility, and all of this even while you were on the way of the virtues. Do this and you shall see how great is my love for you.

My Daughter, this is the greatest blessing which I dispense upon my little children and it is so for many reasons.

The first reason is that as Creator and Lord, having fashioned this creature so that it could love and serve me in this world, a creature which then dares to disobey me repeatedly, still I, as Creator and Lord, put up with this iniquity over and over again without vindicating myself and I go on providing all the favors and the services which the nonhuman creatures provide for you for the preservation of your bodily life.

Second, I apply, for your benefit, the Blood of my blessed Son, when I give you the inspiration to receive the sacrament of Penance and make the Redemption efficacious for you and thus assure you, by means of the sacraments, of your eternal salvation and of the eternal kingdom of glory.

...Therefore, love me and thank me today and always for my merciful blessings so that you can always receive an even greater mercy and pardon.

The continual pardoning of offenses for anyone who repents of them from the heart — this makes me recognize God in holiness. One cannot find a greater grandeur in the whole world.

101. Spiritual Exercises for December, med. 15
You must renounce all things visible, sensible, and desirable. You must study my words attentively for they are divine words in which you will attain to the grandest eternal treasures, even here in this exile! This is eternal wisdom!

You must renounce the visible first of all, that is everything in the fabric of this world in which is found earthly and transitory beauty — and it must be a continual renunciation.

At first nothing will pin you down to the allurement of these things because they are vile and because they are not your God. Thus, you shall seem to be like a corpse with no memory of these things at all.

In this way you will renounce all earthly created things, taking no account of anything that happens at the sense level of your own person or of any other created creature. All your passions and their movements will be forgotten and their many variations will have no effect on you; you shall not give in to any of them at all. Your spirit shall remain unmoved, not letting any of them enter into your higher self.

Thus, you shall be renouncing all the appetites and desires and every other affection and inclination of love for any created thing and every created object, even if it be spiritual, but you shall continue loving God alone in all of these creatures.

You shall renounce all thoughts about both temporal and spiritual things that your fantasy proposes and which your intellect would like to examine and know. The only exception is that pure knowledge of faith through which your will puts into practice your love for me.

And if you do this, you shall possess the eternal, invisible Good in such a way that, even though you live in this very changeable world with all its miseries and its constantly changing times, you shall live in the eternal immutability of my very Being, where neither the devil nor your own passions will be able to take away my Peace which shall dwell within you.

Then, firmly established in this Good, you will not care to leave it for any other thing which the devil may propose to you, no matter how important he tries to make it. For example, he might want you to begin to look back into the past to see if you did good or evil or he might tempt you to look into the future to see if you will succeed or not or for some other purpose, good or evil.

Do not trust any of these things but simply renounce all past and future knowledge and leave everything in my hands and all things will fall into place for you for the best purpose!

With faith, believe in me; with hope, keep your every good secure; and love only me, as the Lord of your heart and as the Life in which you live, renouncing and forgetting everything in yourself which is not me!

102. The Little Garden, 13

Make an examen of perfection each day to be a soul faithful to the Lord.

- Have I been exact and diligent in my spiritual exercises and have I performed them with due attention?

- Have I been given to judging my neighbor when such was not my duty since I am not in the office of a superior to the other person?

- Have I taken a vain pleasure in myself because of my good works or because of the graces I have received from the Lord?

- Have I desired to be loved and highly esteemed by creatures or have I been disturbed or resentful at not receiving like honors?

- Have I denied and mortified my sense-appetites in everything that is not purely necessary and have I become as if dead on this earth?

- Have I taken pleasure apart from God and have I loved anything else but him alone?

- Have I been observant in not talking to anyone except when necessary; that is, outside of common recreation and have I, in all things, taken stock of the obligations of my Rule?

- Have I interfered in things which have not been committed to my care and have I given my opinion without being asked for it?

- Have I sought relief for my body without any precise necessity and have I returned thanks to God for the blessings I have received?

- Have I been punctual about silence and have I been willing to suffer anything for God?

- Have I had recourse to the Lord in all my needs and have I desired to see him in heaven?

- Have I stood guard over the slightest movement of self-love and have I resisted it and have I justified myself?

- Have I acted as if God alone were mine and as if all other things were merely created things?

- Have I considered myself to be the least of all creatures and the most ungrateful to the Divinity, and as such, have I desired to be despised?

- Have I done anything without permission and have I obeyed punctually and have I carried out the Divine Will in everything?

- Have I carried out all my works, thoughts, and words in union with the works, thoughts, and words of my Spouse, Jesus Christ, and have I made my dwelling place in his divine and loving Heart?

m. *Humility and Meekness*

103. Rules, Humility, and Meekness, 7r-7v (176-177)

"Learn of me for I am meek and humble of heart" (Mt 11:29).

Humility and meekness of heart are the foundation of Christian perfection and the root of all the other virtues. These two virtues sum up all my divine perfections hidden in the heart of the Divine Father from all eternity.

It is this divine perfection which I want to communicate to everyone. I came down from heaven to give and donate to all humans this divine perfection, that is, to communicate and give to man the true Way to his eternal salvation.

Therefore, I have said: Learn from me because I am meek and humble of heart. I have taught this virtue more by my example than by my words.

The Divine Heart is its own word and is itself Eternal Wisdom. He sent it into the world so as to unite himself with human nature. And this humility was the divine perfection which flowed from God the Father. This process, by reason of which you can say at one and the same time true God and Man is for you both incomprehensible and admirable. Therefore, the Holy Church in profound admiration sings and says: You did not abhor the Virgin's womb.

This was the humility of divine perfection: and this kind of humility no mere human can imitate. However, united to human nature, this Divine Heart of the Father, a loving God, became, in my Humanity, humble and a meek Lamb.

I put myself in the midst of wolves-sinners so that you might imitate me in this excellent virtue and divine perfection. Out of love for you, I was willing to suffer insults, calumnies, blasphemies, envy, vituperation, spitting, flogging, and an ignominious death as a criminal and this, without opening my mouth in laments or self-defense, leaving myself in the power of the wicked, so that I might do their good pleasure.

I was that Lamb which John saw assisting at the throne in the midst of those animals, the

Lamb being paid homage by an innumerable crowd, to whom the Father has given all honor and glory as to the very Heart which came out of the Father's breast, where all his infinite pleasures are found. Therefore, as truly meek and humble of heart and recognizing myself as Man, with no regard for my Divinity, and as one worthy of this kind of suffering since I took upon myself all the faults of men and like a sinner was obliged to make satisfaction to the Divine Justice for the sins of men. And he looked upon me on the cross as a debt-ridden man.

And thus it is that I ask you to have a real knowledge of who you are. And that which I have done for you out of love and not out of necessity, you also should do out of justice, recognizing yourself in truth for what you really are, both because of the effects of original sin within you and because of your personal sins which you have committed.

Therefore, my Divine Heart must remain united to your heart if you are to be truly humble and meek of heart, content to love insults and calumnies without anger or complaints, preferring dishonor to honor and revilement and the disapproval of men to praise, always with honey in your mouth and my Peace in your heart. May God be glorified. Amen.

104. Rules, Constitutions, 23v-24r (177)

This rule primarily requires humility of heart, which is the same thing as being in spirit and truth, that is, in a true knowledge of yourself and of your own proper nothingness and worse than nothing because of your own personal sins.

And any virtues and gifts of God which you have in your soul must be recognized in their original source, namely, God.

In substance, fervor in this particular virtue can go to extremes without you thinking that you are doing something great because any humility that you might practice can never be compared to the profound humiliations of the Son of God.

105. The Little Garden, 12
Receive with humility all the encounters that you may have with contempt and dishonor since I have suffered the pain of the sin of man without any complaint in my Person.

And therefore consider all that is yours as nothing and when humiliations do come receive them with meekness; and let your features be sweet and benign and sympathize with your neighbor's miseries just as I did.

Do not show disdain for anyone; for all creatures were created in my image and likeness but show them *respect and reverence as temples of the Holy Spirit.*

Look upon your superior as the very person of God and look at your sisters as if they were the holy apostles, and in all your community meetings *I shall be there among you.*

106. Rules, Idea, 2r (156)
Let there not be among you any distinctions of honor or precedence after the fashion of worldlings, but let all be united in both mind and heart, united to Christ their Head.

And just as I love you in a most perfect divine charity, so also let all of you love one another in one spirit and one love.

Whoever among you has any ambition to be the greater will become the least! And therefore let there be no incitement or desire for honor or precedence in your hearts; indeed, that one shall be the greater who is more able to embrace the opprobrium and humiliations of her life.

107. Colloquies II, 11 (16)
Know that it is necessary that you suffer many humiliating things from creatures so that in this way you may come to purify anything of self-love that is still within you and also so that your life may be like unto mine.

However, never be silent about the truth when you know it just to avoid the dirty looks of creatures, since telling the truth always gives me glory. Do not get involved in the intrigues of human and transitory things and do not think highly of those things which the world values, such as honors, noble birth, and riches; do not put anyone on a pedestal in your heart because of these things! Be a friend of the poor and of the lowly and do not look down on anyone because of their seeming insignificance, because in my kingdom, the greatest are those who have loved me the most!

My great ones are those who are the more despised and the more humiliated of this earth. The beautiful people and the geniuses without humility are the self-panegyrists of the world. I very seldom remain in "their" hearts because I cannot live there since there is no room for me in their puffed-up hearts which are full of pride and self-esteem. Their mouths often erupt with words of disdain for others and in their intellect, they are full of human laws.

108. Colloquies III, 19 (29)
My Daughter, know that in the Divinity there is a true humility which is on an equal footing with my grandeur. This virtue existed from all eternity in my very nature and being. I produce it in the Word.

...In my very own Mother, whom I chose, I was conceived in the very same act which was communicated to her in the descent of the Word into her womb, that is, by the Spirit uniting Mary's will to the Word's own humility, with her responding with those words: "Behold the handmaid of the Lord." In this way the humility of the Word became the humility of the Mother, and in that very instant I was conceived in soul and body, in the very womb of this Virgin.

Behold how, in the bosom of the Father as God and in the womb of my Mother as man, I was the principle of humility.

And the principle of purity is in proportion to the principle of humility.

109. Colloquies VIII, 82 (92)
My Daughter, you ask me for the virtue of humility. You will enjoy the fruits of this virtue when you practice the upright intention which we treated above.

This upright look with which man gazes upon me is an exercise that completes all the grades of true humility, because all the levels of humility are a practice of authentic truth.

Look at the first level of humility which is your own nothingness, something that is found in the upright intention when you see me and not yourself in all that you do.

The second level of humility is when you see your own misery and vileness inasmuch as you are a sinner and thus worse than nothing.

The third level consists in not desiring the honors and esteem of men but rather abhorring and despising them. This is involved in the notion of rectitude, because uprightness involves hating and despising all that is not the true Good which I alone am.

The fourth level of humility loves the confusions and the insults and enjoys being belittled. This, too, is part of the upright intention, because it unites you to the Life which my Humanity lived on earth and it is toward this alone that every intention which seeks my glory is directed.

The last and most perfect humility consists in giving me all honor and glory and in referring every grace and honor back to me.

110. Colloquies IX, 108 (112)
Oh my Daughter, the Word signifies truth and it is through this truth that I walked

about the streets of this world, speaking to my disciples, and I spoke to them only in terms of truth. I did this because humility seeks to proclaim truth and justice, an attribute proper to the Divinity.

This truth was hidden for all eternity in the bosom of my Father and in his Word. It had not yet entered this world until I came to take on human flesh. I came to make known the truth, the truth of my very being just as it was, and it had a grandeur that was rooted in God's own perfection together with all the perfections of the virtues as they exist in God. God's truth has nothing to do with that false grandeur described by the infernal serpent.

The truth revealed to you concerns my very self, a truth which touches upon the very being of creatures, precisely as creatures, whose humanity I took on, and in doing so I was humbled as Man even to the point of the self-emptying which made me the most abject of all men. It was in this way that the truth of my being as God and the truth of your being as man appeared here on earth among you.

111. Colloquies IX, 119 (119)

In this Holy Communion you show me how you are that most vast sea of perfect and infinite Good and how I am like a drop of water which falls into you and is changed in that vast sea, where losing my own being, I see myself become an ocean of every kind of good. Consequently, losing any sense of my own limited and miserable being and of my littleness, I now feel myself to be a new being, vast and divine, in which I feel no more fear nor the limitation of time. Indeed, in this new state I am like a force, a power, and infinite greatness and an unlimited goodness.

112. Degrees of Prayer III, 18 (7)

Among all the blessed happiness which the heavenly spirits enjoy, the greatest and most essential happiness consists in their being able to see that their God and their very principle, being, and life, is that apart from him they have no being, no principle, no happiness.

Therefore all the glory of the heavenly citizens consists in a true annihilation. It is this truth which makes them happy; since they share in his being they share his beatitude.

Oh God, how can one ever explain something so hidden and secret but nonetheless an infallible truth? What else is the glory of all the saints in heaven but this total annihilation?

Only the saints can be truly humble, not we poor pilgrim creatures. And the reason is because they know themselves in the light of an unveiled truth, clear and without any cloudiness or any other obstacle, in such a way that they see that God alone is the cause and the principle of their being and of their every good.

113. Degrees of Prayer III, 20 (8)

Our dear God...by means of a revealed faith shows the soul how he is the all within the being of everything.

And this reflection destroys everything that is false, deceptive and untruthful in man when he sees the things of this world on the same level as he himself, and this in turn arouses an act of annihilation in terms of all created things, and even of the self.

In such an act, the human spirit finds its very center and discovers the truth it wanted, like one traveling on the road toward its principle, which is its being and its own good, and there experiences and feels within itself a marvelous happiness, as if it were discovered in its own nonbeing.

114. Spiritual Exercises for December, med. 2

My Daughter, here is your mistake, namely, that you spent too many years of your life without this self-annihilation, you have made yourself an unreal being, charmed by your own shadow, attributing to yourself omnipotence, wisdom, and goodness.

...Goodness, because you loved yourself, looking on my gifts and my goods produced in you by me, as if they were yours and as if your good works would serve to bring you your self-esteem in your created being, and you turned to your natural gifts and blessings to fashion for yourself a high throne of your being with a vain trophy to yourself...and there you also sought to evilly sanctify your own being by your self-adulation.

From all of this you will see the great necessity of walking the road of true self-annihilation. And this is the way of truth, and the secure way on which the soul is freed from its mistakes as also from the mistakes of the devil, the world and the flesh, and permits you to fly with the wings of my grace on the way of perfection. Therefore, annihilate yourself in your very being.

115. Spiritual Exercises for December, med. 3

Behold, my Daughter, what kind of grace, so great and rich in blessings, was given for your benefit alone so that you could rise to the all! But I advise you never to forget the nothingness that you really are on your own if you wish to possess that All which I am even without you.

Here is where the great truth lies. You should praise and thank me for so many gifts: I have given you an excellent being, with both the experience and the remembrance of your nothingness. This truth should be the foundation of an ever-growing self-annihilation in my sight in both your work and true activity. Thus, you will be grateful for this truth.

116. Exercises of Love for Every Day, February 5

The Divine Spirit breathes in him so as to form in Jesus Christ the solid foundations of the Catholic Church, his Spouse, in which he is the cornerstone on which he would necessarily fashion a magnificent and stable edifice, profound and marvelous in its beauty and divine magnificence.

This chosen cornerstone, planted within the depth of the divine essence, was chiseled and produced by the hands of the divine Artisan well disposed for providing within it a fundamental structure, one hollowed out of the deepest limit of an excellent humility. There, like a living Rock carved out with the hard blows of all kinds of suffering, it produces many other stones in this magnificent edifice of the living Temple of the true God. The Man-God was that great rock laid by the Divine Father for this very edifice here on earth. And it was the Man-God who, by the blows of the omnipotent Artisan, was designated and fashioned in an extraordinary profundity in true and excellent humiliations which were rooted at the very center of the Divinity, with such a solid foundation, so that as a result he would be able to build not a material temple like Solomon's, which cannot even be compared to the temple which is the Church militant in its many riches, its magnificence and its beauty. The former, that is, Solomon's temple, was a vile richness formed of earth and lowly material, subject to decay and death, the latter's preciousness and magnificence was built of living, precious stones.

...The Holy Spirit formed the Man-God's humanity in the womb of Mary because it was from this Humanity that everything else would be sculptured as complimentary to such a magnificent edifice.

117. Exercises of Love for Every Day, April 12

The soul, with all its annihilations, seated in your presence, Word-God, admired and at the same time forgetful of itself wishes no other food than your most pure glance. And the sweet companionship which it enjoys takes away any desire for earthly food.

There you invite the loving soul with a hunger and an appetite to satiate itself with your humiliations and to feed itself on the divine works and on the fullness of those goods which the soul fully discovers therein, drawn as it is by your glance of love. And the soul is wounded by the two lights of your most pure eyes, namely, humility and love, that is, the humility of the Divine Word and the love that caused your own humiliations.

Oh how wonderful to sit in your presence with the soul forgetful of everything and wishing that you consume it and satiate it with your humiliations and your love. Here are those burning desires which, like a flame, burn the heart of love, but a pure love of making oneself like unto the Beloved.

However, because the soul is always fired-up more and more, you look upon her and cause her to experience your divine gaze and you allure her by saying: Where shall we have enough bread to feed your hunger, that is, how shall you be able to attain and satiate yourself with opprobria and the cross and suffer for love of me as I did for you? How can you ever humiliate yourself for me as much as I did for you since I am God and you are a vile creature, a vile sinner from whence are born all sorts of pride and so many vices, all so very unlike me? Your humiliations are due to you and mine were done by a Divine Person.

O my Love's Word, if I were able to know and understand who you are then I would know and be capable of understanding what kind of humiliations you suffered.

...The desire which you have enkindled in my soul with the light of your pure eyes has filled me; your glory is made manifest in my soul in your humiliations and your abjections. There one tastes your amiable thirst, so sweet and delightful and admirable and full of mercy! In your humiliations all the riches and the sweetnesses of your infinite glory are hidden.

How can I ever thank you for these marvelous humiliations while you invite me to keep you company and you in your mercy deign to gaze on me with your divine light.

n. *Love of the Cross*

118. Rules, Love of the Cross, 9r-9v (188-189)

"If anyone wishes to come after me, let him deny himself, take up his cross each day and follow me" (Lk 9:23).

Every soul which denies its own will is immediately united to my Divine Will and becomes a spouse of the Cross.

Just as I never followed my own will but only the Divine Will and just as I espoused myself to the cross on Calvary, so too all my chosen souls, by embracing my cross and denying their own will, bind themselves to the Divine Will and unite themselves to my own Divine Delight.

Oh with what love I embraced the cross, loved it, desired it, and took pleasure in it — all for your love.

Likewise, those who love me bind themselves to the cross and rest thereon, like a spouse who rests on the nuptial bed.

They love the fatigues, troubles, pains, and the insults of creatures, the interior derelictions, the sorrows; they love sickness more than health and it is the same with spiritual consolations. They even love death to the self more than life itself. Finally, they love the cross just as I have loved it and, in this way, they attain the perfect union of the soul with God.

In this way the soul makes the Divine Will its own, being dead to its own will. Then they savor the true and solid sweetnesses of God and the true peace found therein. And the soul which experiences this will understand it all.

Such souls now enjoy nothing at all except to see themselves on the cross.

Therefore, if you really want to imitate me with that more perfect love which I have for the Father, then love, with all your heart, the sufferings and all the crosses and troubles of life which he might be pleased to send you. Do this, not only to obtain your eternal crown but also that you might be so many living images of my Humanity.

119. Rules, Constitutions, 27r-27v (186)

It is impossible that a soul be joined to an authentic imitation of our Lord Jesus Christ and to the perfect observance of these Rules and Constitutions unless it first embraces in its life the cross and renounces its own will in everything so as to carry out the Divine Will.

Just as our Lord Jesus Christ did in his most holy life, so also he summons the soul to his food, saying: "My food is to do the will of him who sent me." In the Garden of Olives, praying to his Father, he said: "Not my will, but thine be done!" This is the way it was both at the beginning and the end of his most precious life.

Therefore, whoever wishes to attain a true union with and likeness to this divine Christian Exemplar must have the courage and a magnanimous spirit and be resolved to abandon all things which might be an obstacle to this great good by denying his own will and by not making any peace with his own self-love but continually battle self because this is what all the saints did to attain this goal.

Consequently, they shall love and have a great regard for everything that in religion is more difficult and arduous for their own will and their sensuality. They shall accept with love sickness, troubles, and crosses; internal spiritual desolations; and all losses as means of salvation sent to them by the Heavenly Father to make them true and living and original images of his Beloved Son.

120. The Little Garden, 12

You shall live a life of constant dying to yourself in everything you do and in this you shall be exact and diligent, crucifying yourself on my cross and living crucified in my holy Flesh, putting aside totally the old man and getting rid of all your carnal-sensual activity so as to live in the New Man, Christ, the Man-God, your Spouse.

121. Autobiography, 82 (159)

You are my friend and my delight and, therefore, I keep you in my kingdom of the cross and of glory, in the kingdom of my peace and rest, in sufferings and afflictions, just the way I lived as a pilgrim on this earth.

And now I conform for you this new Institute which he has given you. And he said: "Do not be troubled, you already know how much you have to destroy the self so that this Work may be carried out and, therefore, it is necessary that you suffer and deny yourself, so that you can be buried, as it were, in suffering and self-annihilation so that only everything which is mine might remain in you." This is exactly what I told and showed you at the start of this Work — namely, that this Work is totally mine.

122. Colloquies VI, 48 (63)

Do not be displeased when you are despised and contradicted; know that this is my pleasure. Love me alone and do not be concerned about any other. You have received the three jewels of pure love, disdain, and the cross. And how do you expect to enjoy their fruits except in the very same way I enjoyed them here on earth? These are my treasures which I let my chosen ones share. So stop thinking of yourself. These treasures belong to you.

123. Colloquies VIII, 74 (86)

I have built my kingdom on sufferings as the King of sorrow so that I might give you the kingdom of eternal happiness.

Give your attention to the treasure that I disclosed to you on the cross in which the eternal glory is enclosed. My true and faithful servants have wept and sighed night and day so that I might make them worthy of my kingdom of the cross. And you, what are you doing to receive these blessings which I am granting you? Surely because of your sins you have not merited these treasures which I disclose to you. Therefore, thank me for such a good and always reflect during your whole life on this fact; namely, that you did not merit to gain in your soul these treasures of my Kingdom of the Cross — a fruit which I give only to my friends.

Meditate day and night on this desire which I have to see you with me on the cross, crucified to self-love, honor, and pleasure.

Just as much as you bind yourself to me, your highest Good, so just will you be bound to the cross, held and embraced by me, hating your own self-love and condemning, along with every taste for evil so that you can unite yourself to your only Good.

124. Colloquies VIII, 77 (88)
When you behold me on the cross, hanging there above the earth, remember how you yourself must live in this world, nailed along with me by three nails, that is, the contempt of creatures, contempt of oneself, and contempt for every consolation.

125. Colloquies IX, 111 (114)
My Daughter, know that in this world you will never be separated from my Passion and

that you will have an abundance of troubles and infirmities because you cannot dedicate yourself to love without suffering. This is the way I have arranged it and together with you *all is love!*

126. Colloquies IX, 113 (115)

If I fall beneath my weaknesses and miseries, you help me by giving me a living confidence in you, and you stretch out your loving hand and protect me with your eyes of Divine benignity and I turn to my Good.

If you afflict me with troubles, persecutions, and sufferings from other men and from creatures, you also comfort me with your voice of Truth deep within me. You revive me for more suffering, reminding me that your life in this world was just like this so that you might fulfill your Father's Will.

...And if the devil attacks me with fierce and brutal suggestions, assaulting my soul and body and stirring up all my passions, you present me, O Lord, with a passive act of pure faith, so obscure and yet at the same time luminous by which, according to your Divine Will, you support me with unending patience during every action of the enemy. As a result, I am committed to live, even for a thousand years, suffering whatever you wish for me.

...You are with me in my sufferings. Indeed you are my sufferings, my troubles, and my pleasure as well. However, both the trouble and the pleasure are undertaken so that I might, in turn, abandon them for my only and dear God and that is you, my Love, every breath that I take is breathed in and out on the Loving Cross of the God-Man.

127. Colloquies IX, 116 (117)
Your humanity was crucified on the cross of the Word made Man, your God, that is, it is perpetually on the cross and always united to the joy of my Divine Spirit.

...Listen to me on the Cathedral of the Cross, which I have placed in your heart so that I may live my life in you as a pilgrim, crucified in this world. You shall see me in your spirit, crucified on the bare cross of poverty, crucified in your body with the weakness of sickness, crucified in your spirit in your aridity, dereliction, and melancholy, your weariness and bereft of any consolation. And I shall bring this about in such a way that everything will be for you both a cross and peace as also for me, a pilgrim.

...*Gaze* upon me with a look of the love crucified in you. You shall always behold this sight for it is in this way that I give you my compassion just as the Father is pleased in me.

128. Colloquies IX, 126 (123)
My Daughter, if you really want to have liberty and an unshakable peace of mind inasmuch as this is possible in this valley of tears, never really troubled, then live with a burning desire to attain the ultimate in suffering in this exile with every kind of suffering, that is, sickness, desolation, abandonment, poverty, temptations, dishonor, persecutions, derisions, mockery, insults, contempt, and with

the desire that everyone in this world be there for no other reason than to afflict you with every kind of suffering and travail.

Nourish your spirit in love with this kind of desire so that you may become a living likeness of me in your own being. Nourish your soul day and night with this kind of hunger and desire. Let your food be this love and when you are finally joined to your final homeland, you shall see that it is there that you will find both joy and true repose in the eternal beatitude of heaven.

But even here as a pilgrim you shall experience how much you are capable of, because no matter what the cross may be, the tribulation or the suffering by which you are tried and purged in this life are all ordained by me for your greater good and are, in the final analysis, less than you desired for making yourself like unto your Original, and less than that hunger which your love and desire produce in your spirit. And when you see yourself unworthy to possess the highest degree of suffering, then you shall have, because of this, more suffering in a consuming love where everything you suffer will seem like nothing at all!

...There you shall savor true humility, in the love and union with my Divine Father, in the joy of the Holy Spirit, in spirit and in truth, united to that most perfect living out of the last periods of my life, that is, when I was consummated as a holocaust on the Cross, sacrificing myself to the Father in the fire of this pure love, a perfect love for both him and my souls.

129. Degrees of Prayer XI, 90 (36)

The most Sacred Humanity, since it had the highest kind of knowledge, was always stretched out on the cross alive. But my most Holy Soul was likewise always on the cross, however, it was also in glory at the same time by reason of its participation in the joy and union of the Divine Word.

And this was the greatest miracle of all, namely, that the Divine Omnipotence operated in the Man-God who was a pilgrim uniting in him at one and the same time the greatest suffering and the greatest glory plus the greatest and most perfect love in the act of fulfilling his Divine Will.

Thus it is, that in this kind of prayer the soul sees, or to put it in a better way, the soul is placed in the very presence of this most pure Mirror. And with just one glance it sees distinctly all these divine actions in its beloved crucified Jesus. And there, it sees them all at one and the same time and enters with love and is united to all his sufferings and joys together. Everything takes place at one time and the soul is filled with joy and with a most intense love as it is surrounded totally by sorrows and sufferings and becomes like unto that likeness which is focused and impressed in its soul like a seal impressed in soft wax.

130. Spiritual Exercises for December, med. 17

Jesus wishes his likeness in the love and in the desire for suffering and in the actual suffering that happens in the soul of his spouse.

My Daughter, today you shall treat of the likeness of love in which every good will be given you.

Always look upon your God-Man who was such a friend of suffering and see in his words how he desired to be baptized, which he wanted with a great desire. And he was talking about his death on the cross with all its pains and sorrows, its contempt and torments, which he had to suffer for men, right up to Calvary.

Throughout his whole life, his heart was always on fire with the desire of seeing himself embracing the cross.

It is here that you must long to see yourself on the cross with a desire to suffer without any inclination for any joy at all. You must desire the cross and the sufferings, eager to see yourself on Calvary with my Son, your God, transformed in a true union and a true likeness unto your Lord in a purity of love in which all your passions are purged and every rebellious sense is made subject to your mind's dominion.

There you will find true liberty and true glory where like a queen you shall be in possession of the kingdom of your King. No obstacle shall take away the true peace of the just and you shall conquer all your enemies.

Day and night set afire within yourself this desire; feed your spirit on this kind of love and nourish your soul on this bread of a hungering for suffering every kind of pain, sorrow, revilement, and all sorts of crosses and a hunger to see yourself on Calvary, crucified and derelict even unto the ultimate in suffering. And no matter what encounter with suffering you may see in your life, you shall suffer it with perfect patience, because it will always be less than you desired since your desire was to see yourself as a likeness of my Son.

And with this desire you shall conquer your senses and your passions in such a way that you will render yourself beautiful and pure in my sight, because in you I shall behold an authentic likeness of my Beloved Son, a likeness which I shall be pleased and delighted with for all eternity.

And you shall be exalted and glorified because of this, and you shall be drawn from the earth far and beyond every human understanding. And there you shall see things never seen before, things beyond the senses. You shall understand in a way you never understood before. There you shall possess pure love, and your glory will be beyond measure where you shall behold the likeness of your God within you and you shall live in him through love itself.

131. Exercise of Love for Every Day, April 4

God the Father brings me back to life again in you and he vivifies me with your death.

Oh most precious death which has brought me back to life! Thus, you divine loving Word, my Love, you give life to those to whom you wish to give life. However, just as your Father did not revive us before your most sad death, so you also did not bring the soul this precious resurrection until the soul first dies to all the life of the interior and exterior senses, because you wish that the soul move through your dying, where it must revive to a new life of love in you the Word and Life of everything.

Here you put the soul into atrocious interior sufferings in an admirable and divine way as will be said elsewhere when the course on your Passion will be treated. Here it is sufficient to note those who are the dead whom the Father has resuscitated in you, and how they have been vivified after the death to the senses had been effected in us as it was in you.

o. *Fraternal Community*

132. Colloquies IX, 93 (100)
Look upon your neighbor with the same love with which I regard my disciples and apostles. With this glance of love, you will look upon those companions with whom you live. With my pity, you shall have compassion on them in their weaknesses; with my charity, you will console them in their anguish; with my sweetness, you will speak to them about things of the eternal kingdom; with my sufferings, you shall suffer the movements of their nature. Never use on your neighbor the language of violence in any kind of situation so that you may fulfill in yourself that which was written about me: "Honey and milk on his tongue." Let your words be words of sweetness and love.

133. Rules, Daily Exercises, 2v-4v (160 ff)
As soon as they rise from sleep, let them

thank me for all the blessings received and for having protected them from the snares of the enemies while they were asleep.

Then let them offer me the firstfruits of their affections and the possession of their hearts. Let them unite their thoughts and all the faculties of the soul to my spirit and to the glory of the Eternal Father. Let them offer him all the words, actions, and sufferings of the day, abandoning themselves into his Divine and blessed hands. Then, let them recite the Our Father, Hail Mary, and the Creed and let them not leave their room without asking the blessing of my dear Mother.

When the bell sounds, they shall all gather in the choir to recite Matins of the Divine Office and they shall recall the truth and the prophecies and figures of the Old Law which apply to my Person and are verified in my Life in the New Law of grace.

At the end of Matins and Lauds, which are all songs of praise for the benefits bestowed on the world, the one who takes my place shall intone the Come Holy Spirit as a *memorial* of the hour of my Incarnation, because at that hour the sunrise of the Divine Sun rose upon the world and warmed on the earth the dew of the grace of the Holy Spirit on my creatures.

Then they shall read the Holy Gospel, following it with a meditation on the reading. After this, a virtuous practice shall be proposed for practice during that day, along with the exercise of the holy virtues. Then they shall recall the Work which the Holy Spirit performed at the hour of my Incarnation with my human nature.

...Terce shall be recited with the greatest devotion possible since that was the hour when the Holy Spirit fired up my apostles and the faithful.

...Sext shall be recited as a *memorial* of the preaching of my apostles, after which they received the Holy Spirit and then, in turn, all those things that they preached as they confessed my Name throughout the world and paid its price in their own life.

Tell them that they shall enjoy the fruits of my Presence for one entire hour....The holy sacrifice of the Mass shall be celebrated as a *memorial* of my Passion and Death. The whole community shall assist at this action...at this time of grace let them stand with attention and profound reverence so as to receive the fullness of the heavenly treasures in their minds and let fall upon their hearts the abundance of my mercies, like the dew falling on the meadow, by participating in the justice and truth of my Spirit.

When these activities are over, they shall retire to their own jobs, their hearts united to my Heart, and let all of their works, thoughts, and words be done with uprightness and truth so that they might know that I live in them and they live in me.

At the hour of None, when the bell rings, all shall go into the choir to praise me and they shall remember the great sermon which I gave just before the Last Supper with my apostles....The examination of conscience shall be made as a *memorial* of that examination of conscience my apostles made when I told them that one of them would betray me and each of them said: "Is it I, Lord?"

Then all shall recommend themselves to my Mother's intercession with her litany so that they may protect their souls from sins and from the snares of the infernal enemy. They shall also recommend all their spiritual and temporal needs to her as true children of their dear Mother so that she might protect them as she did my apostles to whom I entrusted her as the Dispenser (of all graces) after I left the world.

Let them go to meals with thoughts of the Last Supper which I had with my disciples.

...Some spiritual reading shall be done as a *memorial* of those discussions I had while I ate with my disciples. At the meal's end, they shall give thanks just as I did at the end of the Last Supper.

...For one hour they shall give some relief to the body by uniting in a holy happiness and charity among themselves; however, during this time (of recreation) this activity should not alienate them from me. This is the way I acted with my disciples so that they would not be accused of what was said of my enemies: "This is your hour and the power of darkness" (Lk 22:53).

A signal for the Three Hours Silence shall be given in *memory* of the three hours in which I hung on the cross and suffered for the salvation of the human race.

...A sign for the beginning of spiritual reading shall be given which shall last for half an hour to signify that the book of the cross contains the teaching of all Christian books and virtues.

There shall then be a half hour of mental prayer as a *memorial* of the prayer which I made to my Father for those who crucified me, wherefore you should also pray in this hour for all those souls who are now crucifying me in this world in their own hearts by their sins. In this way you shall also have a part in the work of salvation which I performed for the benefit of men.

Vespers shall be in *memory* of my sad death and the psalms in memory of my wounds. The chapter and the hymn shall be in memory of my crowning with thorns and the canticle of the *Magnificat* in honor of the sufferings and sorrows which my dear Mother suffered at my death, under the cross.

...They shall dedicate their work of manual labor as a *memorial* of the hours which I hung dead on the cross.

They shall say Compline with great devotion in *memory* of my burial.

...There shall also be a half hour of mental prayer in *memory* of the time in which I spent praying to my Father, during the nighttime in the deserted mountains, praying for the fullness of his mercy for all my souls so as to leave the world an example of the importance of this particular exercise.

...In the intervals...they shall remember the sadness and the dispersal of my disciples and apostles, rendered like a flock without their Shepherd.

During the evening meal, they shall read something, just as they did in the morning, to remind them of the evangelical needs which my Word has planted in the hearts of my disciples and apostles, because at the coming of the Holy Spirit these needs, which are my Words, which I have sown in the hearts of my disciples and apostles, shall take root and multiply a hundredfold for the benefit of all my Church.

After supper they shall give me the usual thanks.

Then they shall gather together for recreation and rest, with devout and holy discussions and holy joy and this, as a *memorial* of the spiritual consolation which I had with the holy Fathers in limbo, when after my death I went there to free them from their dark prison. Toward the end of recreation, a sign shall be given for the obedience, and the one who takes my place shall announce to all the sisters those for whom they shall apply their good works of the following day.

The Great Silence shall last from evening until the following day, and it shall be as a *memorial* of the hidden life and the silence which I experienced for thirty years of my life from my birth, hiding at that time the magnificence of my divine being in my Humanity.

At the times in which silence is not prescribed, they shall remember the three years
during which I opened my mouth to preach
the eternal truths. Just as the light of the
world is brightest at midday, so also the last
three years of my life were days of light and
clarity for the world. In line with this idea,
the religious, at those times when silence is
not prescribed, shall make sure their words
are directed to my greater glory just as everything I did was directed to the glory of my
Eternal Father.

...Make it clear that the evening silence shall
be a thanksgiving to my Eternal Father for
having given me to the world. And they
shall thank him for all the graces and the
treasures which the Church enjoys through
my merits.

...The religious shall make an evening examination of conscience and shall give thanks
for the blessings received, and the one who
takes my place shall give all of them a blessing in my name.

Before going to bed they shall ask for my
dear Mother's blessing.

134. The Little Garden, 10
My Daughter, listen to the voice of my
Purity, hear how you are to comport yourself
in those two actions which you have to perform to give your body and your senses
some rest, actions in which there is always a
danger of some excessive complacence in
them, namely, eating and recreation.

In these acts, you shall leave your senses so disinterested that the necessity of these acts should be your motive in performing them, leaving your spirit united with your God in love, without leaving your nest and your cell empty, but you should rather feed on my Spirit more than the body feeds on bodily food.

Go to recreation with a gentle and serene spirit and perform all you do there for the good of your neighbor. Let the least word you speak be spoken in a spirit of purity and simplicity. Do not stop to judge your neighbor's activity. Do not expose any vain happiness and do not leave that Beloved cell which is my Divine Heart. Always try to introduce useful and virtuous conversations so that I may dwell in the midst of you. If anyone else introduces worldly conversations, do not answer in any way and if you can, try to head off such discussions and do not speak of such things yourself. Recreation is not the time to discuss the affairs of the monastery unless this is required of you by holy obedience, and if such should be the case let it be done with diligence and punctuality.

III. FIDELITY TO PROFESSION

135. Spiritual Exercises for December, med. 13

Of the great blessing of one's vocation and of the obligations of a spouse who has betrothed herself to a God — on purity of life.

My loving Daughter, what thanks you should give me for the blessing of your religious vocation!

You are one of the few who have been chosen and destined to enter into the promised land of the religious life. From numerous people, only seven were chosen from all the Israelites to enter the Promised Land; in the same way, only a few are chosen from the vast number of seculars in this world to enter into the Promised Land of the religious life, a land so fertile and so abundant. Those who do enter are lead like queens to possess the kingdom of their King. However, before they are received as spouses, they are led to a chosen place where they first of all must purify themselves of any stain or flaw of ugliness. And then, adorned and clean they appear before the King in all their beauty. With the three vows of poverty, chastity, and obedience they become fit for the union already referred to.

By the vow of poverty they are stripped of all earthly goods, by chastity they are pure and cleansed, beautiful in my divine eyes; by obedience they are stripped of their own will because only the Will of their Spouse lives in them.

You have already attained these goods and these blessings of my mercy. See now if they have borne fruit, namely, those obligations which are sought after in these sacred vows; that is to say, has the vow of poverty really stripped you of all human property so that you hate every satisfaction and convenience, loving only true poverty, humble and despised. In terms of chastity, have you been stripped of every creaturely affection no matter how holy it may seem, making sure that your eyes look upon nothing for the sake of satisfying your own liking. Are you careful that your ears do not listen to idle words with satisfaction, and your mouth speaks nothing except for God's glory, keeping your senses in check like prisoners. Only mortification will keep this vow of chastity like a most pure lily which, by its scent, refreshes and purifies the soul, making it like an enclosed garden for the delight of the Divine King. It is with the third vow, obedience, that you have denied your own will in everything that my Divine Will has disposed for you in those things where, carrying out such a denial of your will, I have made your will my Will and in this way have joined you to myself in an unending union.

See whether you have observed and carried out all these obligations with a due gratitude for my mercy in choosing you to be among the number of those few souls who enter the promised land of the religious life where my chosen spouses live and where I go to gather my delights among the children of men.

136. Autobiography, 43 (98)

Oh blessed companionship (of the Lord) of the faithful soul! Who can be afraid of making such a choice in this world?

Oh if only we had this living faith in our spiritual and temporal needs we would never lose heart in the troubles which occur in this miserable life.

I have experienced this myself: a strong shield against all my enemies, and not only this but also a Liberator, a defender in every kind of evil. It is truly a possessing of every good for the soul who puts its trust in him.

Ah! He is my Father and my Mother and he alone is my Being and my Life.

137. Colloquies VIII, 80 (91)

For the soul who is dedicated to this uprightness (even if it is acquired only by its cooperation, and then, later, by the gift of my grace), there is a recompense for its fidelity...a rewarding for all of its past diligence, in such a way that even its indifferent actions become sanctified and take on a quasi-infinite value because of the value and the degrees of charity which the soul possesses by reason of the union of the Divine Persons with the soul.

Oh my Daughter, if you could evaluate all

your past actions, all your thoughts, all your words and works, and all the hours and moments of your life, you would be able to see all the goods that you have lost by your carelessness alone, you would die of sorrow!

However, if you could focus your attention on two things: one is the bareness of the movements toward which your heart has been inclined in its works and intentions, and the second is the riches and blessings, the nobility and the excellence to which you were able to ascend if all of the above had been done with purity and integrity.

138. Colloquies IX, 97 (102)

My Beloved Lord and Spouse, you are my only special Friend; so much so that I would not be able to live an hour or even a moment without you! And it seems to me that my spirit now rejoices when it reflects on this, namely, that each day and each hour it gets nearer the eternal possession in the enjoyment of your Divine Face, and this alone saddens my heart, when I feel within myself the slightest movement of the senses or of self-love, even if this happens rarely, I still experience a pain and sorrow like unto death.

My present life appears again to be bitter because of my constant fear of giving you displeasure...my ordinary condition is a seeming out-of-touchness when others speak of you, my true Joy, because my heart suddenly is filled with joy; this also happens when I hear others sing any loving hymns about you — it is then I experience pleasure and contentment.

139. Colloquies IX, 141 (132)
My whole soul is bound to you, my Lord, pledging its fidelity to you. Indeed, every part of my soul is, as it were, filled with an inexplicable hatred of anything and everything that cannot be identified with you, my infinite Good.

However, what good would my desire for you, my Lord, be unless you watch over my poverty in your mercy.

And what a source of amazement and eternal admiration it is for my soul when you flood my soul with your Light and let me see all the marvelous works which your Spirit has already performed in my soul, that is, all those fruits of love and mercy, as you separate within the ground of my soul, the light from the darkness and you do it with no work on my part.

140. Spiritual Exercises for December, med. 9
In the Second Coming, it shall become evident how God became Man; however, in his glory and majesty all his divine operations shall be like brilliant rays since they were performed in a most excellent way by the Pilgrim-Man, namely, that infinite love with which he brought about your salvation, that humility and patience with which he suffered the so many and so ignominious humiliations of his death; plus all those other most

precious works, even the smallest — all done, as he himself tells us, with great virtue.

And then there shall appear the infinite price of the Blood he shed to redeem you, and it shall stand out in majesty amid the clouds of heaven and shall shine like the Sun of Justice in his Eternal Truth.

And at the Second Coming, it shall be clear how this God-Man will judge the world using the Man-God as his standard. All people shall be measured in the light of the stature of his virtue and his justice. This shall be evident in those who will be vindicated because of the way they reproduced and recopied the Man-God-become-a-Pilgrim in their own life, and they shall find security despite their fear, when they receive a favorable sentence at that very instant in which the Judge appears to manifest his virtue to them.

The reprobate souls, however, will be condemned in that very same judgment because that very same Precious Blood shed for them was shed in vain. It shall be made clear, in their case, that they in no way imitated his virtues nor did they observe his teachings nor carry out his works. Therefore, these souls shall be seen as deformed and despoiled of their Original, in whose image they were to live as copies.

And because of this deformity, they shall be — in one instant — condemned by the eternal judge and by their own conscience to an eternal burning in hell. And the greatest suffering of their damnation shall be the power of the Blood of my Son which, by means of this fire, shall burn them with suffering and sorrow for all eternity.

141. Spiritual Exercises for December, med. 11

How beautiful death is after a life lived well, in a life of dying and in a death which brings life.

My Beloved Daughter, death is a dream of peace for just souls because they live in love. It is this love which brings them rest in their dying, and they die of this love in a peaceful, sweet, and gentle death. The reason for this is that the just soul always lives a death-to-self in everything that pleases it and in every disordinate appetite, in every movement of unregulated passion, always denying the acts of its own will so as to carry out the Divine Will and always embracing, while here on earth, every kind of pain and suffering, denying itself and dying to all that pertains to the animal side of life. In addition, it deprived itself of every sort of pleasure, even the most licit, and in this life it constantly lived a daily and hourly dying.

The just soul has no concern over what to eat or what to wear but wants only that which is necessary to maintain its bodily life; it renounces all else and thus it dies by living from moment to moment.

As far as honors and riches are concerned, the just soul acts as if they did not even exist and for this soul life is a constant dying, a living in expectation of death so that it can find that life with which it can truly identify, namely, it awaits its hour of destiny!

And when that hour arrives, there is no *tidings more happy and joyful* for a soul that loves me. This is true not only because the battle is over and because it now leaves behind everything from which it had already separated itself long ago, but it is also a happy message because now this soul is secure and beyond the reach of its enemies. But the greatest source of its contentment at the moment of death is the possession of the Beloved Good, who now lives within the soul in an undying way, as also the possession of the perfection of love experienced by these just souls. It is this fullness of love that brings a death which lets them arise in a full possession of the greatest Good.

And then, the soul, with no more fear, runs to the Eternal Good; its death is but a *most peaceful sleep* in which the soul makes its final journey to its homeland so as to arrive at its true Center in that place where the soul substantially emerges and where it had been generated from all eternity and where it now eternally enjoys him with whom it always desired to be united and wanted to embrace forever.

At death the just soul knows exactly who kills it and who loves it, and the one who loves it will give, along with death, eternal life. That is why the just soul takes *delight* in death at the hands of its Beloved, secure in possessing him through his mercy.

And so, my Daughter, see how beautiful is death for one who has lived always dying! And behold how I lived and you shall see whether your death will be something oppressive or something happy. I lived dying, and it is the *memory (memoria)* of my dying that will be your life.